THE
EYE
OF THE
NEEDLE

DAVID SCHOFIELD

ISBN: 978-1-6847-1633-3 (sc)
ISBN: 978-1-6847-1632-6 (e)

Lulu Publishing Services rev. date: 01/25/2020

CONTENTS

Dedicated to God, His Encourager, and Winston.

ACKNOWLEDGMENTS

I would like to acknowledge Winston, a homeless man who joined my bible study group at an inner-city shelter only hours after being released from the hospital. Winston attempted suicide by drinking a gallon jug of poison. He taught me that it is not that difficult to give up my possessions and follow God.

I would also like to thank a friend I call "the encourager." He is the most genuinely positive person I have ever encountered. His first words when he meets a new person or when just making a passing comment are *always* uplifting, supportive, and encouraging. I was nothing short of stunned by how he engaged with friends, family and strangers. One day, I asked him if he was aware of it. His reply was, "Being encouraging does not cost anything, so why not? It's free."

I have attempted to practice an auto-response of encouragement and it is not something that comes natural to me.

PREFACE

When I was a child, I said the following prayer at bedtime each night:

> Now I lay me down to sleep
> I pray thee Lord my soul to keep
> If I should die before I wake
> I pray thee Lord my soul to take

I felt at peace going to sleep, and I knew with certainty that God was watching out for me. When I woke up, that was another story, and I had to be in charge. Childhood events happened that shaped my beliefs about God, the world, and myself. Some of the events were positive, and others were of a different nature. Consequently, I formed unchallengeable beliefs in early childhood that drove my solutions to situations as an adult. To top it off, these beliefs were hidden from my sight. The hidden and unchallengeable beliefs were formed in this order: I am not good enough; I don't fit in with my peers; and I am on my own.

With this attitude, I set out to succeed in life. A series of events brought me to my knees in my late forties. My solution could only be characterized as self-destruction for my family and me. Thankfully, this plan did not materialize. Instead, I was given a pathway back to God. God did not make the terms too difficult, I just had to be a little willing.

A chain of events occurred that told me with certainty that God cared for, and was watching out for me, as what happened can be explained in no other way. This path ultimately led me to facilitating a bible study on Tuesday mornings at a homeless shelter in the city of Atlanta.

The bible study group consisted of a few volunteers and clients of the shelter sprinkled with homeless individuals that just walked in for the free biscuits and coffee. Winston was one such person.

We were studying a parable called the Rich Young Man. Jesus tells the rich man, "You still lack one thing. Go, sell all your possessions, and give to the poor and you will have a treasure in heaven. Then come, follow me."

Winston spoke for the first time and said, "I gave up all of my possessions for alcohol. I gave up my job, my truck, my wife, my children, and my life. I walked around with a bottle of poison and when I thought about drinking the poison, I would ask myself if I would be okay if this is the last thing I ever see. I guess one day I answered yes to that question, as I ended up in the emergency room from drinking the poison. I have been in Grady hospital for thirty days and was released earlier today."

I asked Winston why it was easier to give up all possessions and his life for alcohol but difficult to do so for God. He said that he did not know but would think about it. Winston came back to the bible study the following Tuesday, and I asked him the same question. Winston matter-of-factly shrugged his reply, "It isn't."

I never saw Winston again, but I knew that I wanted to get to the place that would allow me to give the same answer to that very question.

Others in the group shared that their possessions included anything they had an identity with, as well as where they spent their time. The list was varied: my truck, my job, what people think of me, Facebook comments and likes, watching TV, my bank account, buying on sale, my anger, my children, how my wife looks, gossip, the stock market, my political views, my religion, drinking, fighting, physical strength, anything society says I need, my need to be heard—and this list went on.

I wrote my own list, and I decided to try to give up everything on my list of possessions, anything that I had an identity with. I was not able to make it a week! As Jesus says later in a parable, "What is impossible with man is possible with God." I found this to be true. I could not give up or stop behaviors without asking God to remove my desire to do so. When I stopped spending time on these "possessions" or things that were truly of no value, I found that I had a lot of free time on my hands and intuitively, without effort or intention, began creating new, positive and healthy habits. I was so inspired by Winston's response and the responses of the other men that I decided to write a story about what it might have been like traveling with Jesus and struggling to understand the earthly and divine meanings of his teaching as experienced through the eyes of Andrew, the younger brother of Peter.

In reading the parables in the book of Luke, the Parable of the Sower highlights that Jesus and his followers were supported by women out of their own means. One was Joanna, the wife of Cuza, who was the manager of Herod's household. I had never heard mention of how Jesus and his disciples were fed and supported by women. This story has a lot to do with the women that walked with Jesus as well.

Paul shows up later in my story, and my prayer is that you will discover a way to incorporate one of his teachings into your daily life: "Do not conform any longer to the patterns of this world but be transformed by the renewing of your mind."

I only reference a few of the many teachings of Jesus and Paul. It is my prayer that their words will become a blessing in your life and that you will awaken to your true value and relationship with your creator.

Dave Schofield

ONE

IN THE BEGINNING

I finished my tea and started to daydream, remembering the first day I met Jesus, about three years ago. My name is Andrew, the second and youngest son of Peter. My father was the eldest son of my grandfather, also named Peter. As far back as we know, every male in our family was a fisherman and lived in the same location, if not the same house. Everyone also named their first-born son after themselves. Most men in our family honored the tradition of dying at sea and leaving all their possessions to their eldest son. Dinner conversations usually involved tales of great catches, and I always wondered why we only had one small sailboat. Perhaps it was because father liked wine with his sunsets.

My older brother, Peter, has always been there for me, and I never question him. I did that once, and it did not go so well. He was sure of himself and intuitively knew what to do, especially on the sea. As I grew older and learned the fishing trade, it seemed that Peter did most of the tasks on the boat and usually all of the catching while our father just barked orders. It seemed that Dad liked wine with his fishing as well as with his sunsets.

When I was young, I thought my name was "Hey." Whenever anyone wanted me to do something, they always said, "Hey," and I knew I was being summoned. One day, my brother called me *Andrew*. I will never forget hearing my actual name, *Andrew*. It was about an hour before daybreak on a crisp, clear morning. A cool ocean breeze was rising from the west. The sea fog had lifted, and I had just finished rigging the sails on *Delilah*, our sturdy, unenvied fishing boat that was named after my mother. When I heard my actual name, I knew this was going to be a different day. Peter and I were fit sailors with well-callused hands. I did not see our father and I looked at Peter curiously when he said, "Shove off!"

As we broke through the first waves, Peter declared, "You will be a man tomorrow, so it is time for you to captain!" With that, he sat in the hull and laid down, using fishing line for a pillow. I was nervous but excited at the same time. I would be turning sixteen tomorrow. I had watched my father and brother on many trips to sea. I was to do the tasks of my brother, and my brother was to do the tasks of my father—I hoped without the wine.

Every time I felt unsure and asked a question, Peter replied, "You're the captain!" As the ocean spray hit my face, I knew it would be a glorious and fantastic morning. The gulls did their job guiding *Delilah*, and the hull was full of the best early morning catch we'd had in months. Thankfully, Peter jumped to action when he saw the nets were bulging.

"What's next?" I asked.

He replied, "Take us home, Captain." I grew a little taller that day.

Father saw *Delilah* a long way off and waited on the shore with a wine in his hand. The last time the hull had been so low, the *Delilah* had sprung a leak. His worried expression changed to a laugh when he saw the real reason behind it. The look in Father's eyes made me feel I had somehow crossed over from being a boy into a man—and a fisherman at that! I'd never seen him so proud. He declared, "Andrew is feeding the family." That I was! This was the best day of my young life so far, and it was only eleven thirty in the morning. Father brought us all a little wine to celebrate.

Peter and I were busy laying the fish to dry on the south bank when Peter noticed a man walking along the coastline toward our home. It appeared he was intentionally going nowhere—which is where I felt we lived—or, at least, on the *edge* of nowhere. But this man had a purposeful stride and there was something about him, sure and true. My brother went to talk with the stranger, and I placed the last of the fish in the sun to dry, following him shortly thereafter.

As I approached, I could hear the man ask Peter, "Have you ever met someone and you immediately knew that you should not cross him or her or express defiance?" I thought to myself, *Every week. They are called soldiers with swords.* Then he looked at each of us and paused. "Have you ever met someone who had the answers to all the questions you have not yet asked or even thought of?" The stranger then turned and started walking up the small trail toward the main road, saying only the words: "Follow me."

I watched my brother briefly hesitate, but then walk after him without looking back. Peter had nothing with him but his sandals and the sackcloth he was wearing. He did not even say goodbye to our parents or me. The stranger did not even have sandals. I thought this would be a great afternoon adventure, following a stranger with absolutely no plan. At least I had sandals and a slingshot—and, after all, I will be sixteen tomorrow and had become a man that morning. Little did I know, the choice we made to follow the stranger would alter the course of our lives and those of many others.

I thought we'd be gone for only an hour or two, but we were gone for close to three years.

CHAPTER
TWO

JOANNA, WIFE OF CUZA

J esus, Peter, and I walked the rest of that day, passing various
travelers going both directions. Jesus talked as we walked,
and Peter and I just listened. I realized two things during our
conversation: Jesus knew what he was talking about, and I had no
idea what he was talking about. I slept well that night and, oddly,
was not hungry in the morning, even though we had not eaten the
day before. After two more days of walking, talking, listening, but
not eating, I started to feel a little hungry. It was close to noon,
and I thought we were heading to a small village near Negev, when
Jesus stopped and knocked on the door of the most magnificent
home I had ever seen. It was owned by Cuza. I had heard from

travelers who visited my home that Cuza was a large man with a reputation of respect and was held in high esteem. I was told that if you crossed him, you would only do it once.

My father talked about meeting him once and said that while he was there, he had been served the best wine he'd ever sampled. Cuza's name was well known in my fishing village since he was the manager of Herod's household and holdings, and Herod owned most of the land in the surrounding towns. To my surprise, Cuza invited us into his home to eat and to sit through the midday sun. His young wife, Joanna, and their children joined us for the small feast. I was salivating at the thought of the meal that would soon follow the kitchen's sounds and smells. It would be my first taste of venison; our family meals consisted mainly of fish and mollusks.

While we waited, Jesus spoke. We were all in a trance. "You are the ones who justify yourselves in the eyes of others, but God knows your hearts. What people value highly is detestable in God's sight. No one can serve two masters, either you will hate the one and love the other, or you will be devoted to the one and despise the other. You cannot serve both God and money."[1] He continued, "You cannot serve God and anything, there is only One who is good, and that One is God. For where your treasure is, there your heart will be also, and the mustard seed is all you need."[2]

I started to worry about my life. No one knew what to say or do. The silence was louder than thunder. I thought, *Why in the world would you say, "What people value highly is detestable in God's sight. No*

---

[1] Luke 16:13–15.

[2] Luke 8:34.

one can serve two masters"? Why are you insulting our host? Isn't Cuza the manager of Herod's properties? Herod is Cuza's master. Who in the world did Peter and I decide to follow? I prayed the food would be brought in soon.

Suddenly, and with no explanation, Jesus stood up and said, "Follow me." We were leaving Cuza's home just as abruptly as we had entered. I was annoyed because I had not eaten my dates, let alone bit into my first roasted wild deer. I excused myself, thanked Cuza, and silently prayed he did not kill us on the way out the door.

It was a particularly odd day, and one I could not understand. This day was followed by many others that were puzzling and peculiar only when viewed in retrospect. Jesus did not need retrospect or hindsight.

The day following our almost meal, Cuza's wife, Joanna, caught up with us. When we left their home, it was the second time I'd heard Jesus say to follow him, and I was now wondering if Cuza's wife was supposed to follow us without her husband. I became even more confused when she described her children weeping and begging her not to leave. On that day, Joanna had decided to leave her husband, her children, her home, and everything else she had held dear for so long. When she caught her breath, the next thing she said was something about discovering abundance and not lacking anything for the first time in her life and that she had no regrets. I knew then that she would fit right in; she sounded as confusing as Jesus. His response to Joanna only added to my confusion. Jesus declared that she did not lack anything and lovingly said, "Truly I tell you, no one who has left home or husband or children for the sake of the kingdom will fail to receive many times as much in this age."[3]

We were now a group of four: my brother, Joanna, Jesus, and me. We continued on the road toward Negev. We camped under a mature olive tree that night, and as Joanna gathered the material for a fire and revealed some venison and fresh baked bread, my stomach started to grumble. I was ready for the first of many fine meals to come. Looking back, I am especially grateful for Joanna and the other women who would eventually join us. The men who joined our group seemed to have no money, food, or slaves. I am also grateful to Cuza for letting his wife leave with significant funding. I can only guess that Cuza must have thought Joanna would realize her mistake and would need money to get home. Joanna never returned to her family and kept saying she was home.

---

[3] Luke 18:29.

CHAPTER
THREE

FOLLOW ME

It has been a few years since leaving the fish to dry on the bank next to my parents' house. As I sat remembering that day, I heard the now-familiar words, "Follow me," and Jesus's voice brought me back to the present. His voice is hard to describe and is more like one of those things that can only be experienced. Once it's experienced, it is never forgotten.

Over the coming months, other men and a few women joined our budding group as we traveled from town to village. Thomas was a burly blacksmith. When he heard Jesus's call to follow him, he started to walk immediately, leaving his coals burning. Matthew was a scribe and tax collector, and when he followed, he left the monies he collected and his books where they sat on the table. Luke, a physician and healer, left with patients still waiting. Judas was a famed rabbi and joined us a few minutes before he was supposed to teach a crowd on the sacred texts. I was always surprised at the response to the call to follow, but then again, Peter and I did the same. I never knew or could guess at who in the crowd might truly hear the call, although I tried.

Everyone who joined had one thing in common: they chose to follow Jesus and leave their possessions, identities, and everything else behind. Not one of them remembered to bring food or money, which, as it turns out, is exactly what Jesus had in mind.

From my point of view, without Joanna and the other women, we would not have been able to travel as we did, and many never would have heard Jesus sharing his messages through parables. His teachings would not have spread so rapidly, and there definitely would have been far fewer meals. The women supported Jesus and the rest of us out of their own means. As we traveled from one town and village to another, I imagined what a strange sight we must seem. The people must wonder how Jesus chose his traveling companions and vice versa.

Jesus spent most of his time with the four women: Magdalene, a skilled and sought-after prostitute; Susanna, the great-granddaughter of King Solomon; Susanna's slave, Bathsheba—who made my palms sweat; and Joanna, the beloved wife of Cuza and the mother of Cuza's children. They seemed to have less in common than the men in the group.

As I looked around camp, I noticed there were about fifteen so-called followers now—four women and eleven other men.

At Jesus's words, *follow me*, we broke camp and continued along the dirt road toward the small town of Jerusalem. Jesus did not speak to us directly for most of the day, and everyone stopped asking questions as we traveled. This made the women and me a little uneasy. Questions to Jesus seemed to bring responses that only resulted in more questions. Jesus did not appear to mind my questions when I asked them, and he always guided me to my own answers. His answers always had two meanings—the earthly interpretation and the divine. Even after spending countless nights and days with my teacher and hearing him counsel thousands along the way, I felt that I was only just starting to glimpse the true understanding of his words. Each day began with a new puzzle. Many came to listen to Jesus as we gathered by the river, and they all seemed to want a piece of him—to touch him, to ask a question, or just to be near him. Thankfully, they sometimes brought food and drink in what seemed like payment for his teachings and for being in his presence.

I, too, wanted to be in his presence, and I found myself regularly following him when he left the evening campsite as he had been doing for almost a year. Tonight would be no different: I was preparing to follow him, and everyone else was preparing to bed down by the fire. Although the air was comfortable, the night temperatures could drop rather quickly in the region. Jesus walked away from camp just before the evening meal, seeking solitude to pray. Lately, it seemed that prayer had become as nourishing as food and water to him, and as vital as air. I went after him, but not without grabbing a little food first.

Each day it seemed that Jesus required solitude and prayer more and more often. It was as if he knew a hardship was on the horizon and that he needed strength. From a distance, I watched him walk into an open field. I sat down at the edge of the woods, leaving space between us, and assuming he was unaware of my presence. As I listened to the stillness of the evening and before closing my eyes, I noticed a small herd of deer grazing on the far side of the field near the edge of the pine trees. I lay down, looking at my friend once more. His face seemed empty of all signs of thought or worry—or anything, for that matter. Just being near him, my mind also seemed to relax.

A twig snapped, and a warm breath hit my face. A large buck stood directly over me, exhaling small clouds from his nostrils. I smelled fresh grass and earth on his breath. The buck gave me a curious look and slowly turned to walk into the meadow. Jesus stood over me as well and gazed at the large animal walking away. He then turned and walked toward camp without a word.

I do not remember falling asleep. It was dawn, and there was a dusting of snow on the grass and on me! What a way to start my day. I knew the others must be quite cold, but I felt curiously warm as I followed Jesus back to camp. I could not remember the last time I'd seen him take a meal or drink; nor could I remember ever seeing a man who looked so overwhelmed with abundance and bliss. "Here is a man who has nothing, yet truly lacks nothing.

Everyone he encounters, even the creatures, seem to know him without saying a word," I marveled silently.

I did not smell the familiar fire or hear the usual morning sounds of our group when we got back. The women must not have returned from town. I joined Peter, and we sat against the mature olive tree that had become a trail marker as we traveled the area.

The others were hungry and tired after a disturbing night. Thomas later told me that a column of about one hundred Roman Centurions had marched past our camp in the night. Despite the dusting of snow on his hair and beard, Jesus looked warm and at peace, and he smiled. Peter was the first to greet Jesus on his return, but he did so with a complaint. "We have left all we had to follow you!" he said. "What will there be for us, and when will it happen?"[4]

Jesus smiled as he replied. "Good morning, Peter. It is easier for a camel to go through the eye of a needle than for someone who does not hear and obey to enter the kingdom of God in this age."

I thought it was a little early to start a lesson that only Jesus would understand. "Who then can be successful at this?" I asked. "We have never been able to hear or see, and why do you always say, 'Whoever has ears to hear, let them hear?'"

Jesus replied, "Except you fast to the world, you shall in no way

---

[4] Matthew 19:27.

find the kingdom, and many who are first will be last, and the last first."[5]

I smiled and thought, *This is awesome!* I loved it when Jesus said things only he seemed to understand. Along with the other men in camp, Peter and I began our usual early morning bewildered mumblings, even though Jesus had said the same words to us just about every day for the past three years. I asked the women when the breakfast would be ready, and thus began another typical day.

---

[5] Second Logion; Thomas 27: "Jesus said, 'If you do not fast from the world, you will not find the (Father's) kingdom. If you do not observe the sabbath as a sabbath, you will not see the Father.'"

CHAPTER

FOUR

PURPOSE

E ven though it eluded me, it was obvious that Jesus knew his purpose in traveling with us and that part of his purpose was to help us understand the pathway to our heavenly Father. I could tell he felt confident about the women's understanding of his lessons; they seemed to grasp the divine meaning without explanation. He seemed overly concerned, however, that he might somehow fail the men. He looked at each of us, saying, "You answered correctly only a few weeks ago when I asked, 'Did you lack anything?'"[6]

---

[6] Luke 22:35.

I sipped my tea, listening for the next question or statement that would elude me. It seemed that we lacked everything: we had no money, no houses, no wives (and I had started to want a wife—or at least a girlfriend). We each had only one garment, but Jesus did not even have sandals. I knew that was not the answer Jesus was looking for, so I stayed quiet and listened. No one spoke. Jesus saw our troubled eyes and lovingly said, "You are like the soil along the rocky path—no root—forgetting whose you are."

Typically, one of the women would usually chime in after some silence, but none gave the answer this morning. I asked Joanna why she did not help us understand. She said, "Jesus wants you to see for yourself. He said if you do not discover the answer and rejoice in its discovery, you will never truly believe your answer. Basically, he told us to stop answering for you, as you need to see for yourselves."

There was more tension than usual in the camp this morning. I was not thinking about the answer to Jesus's question; I was thinking about Joanna. By now, I was almost nineteen, a man, and I enjoyed her company. I had yet to experience a woman. I liked hearing people describe my appearance as rugged, but I no longer felt that way. I had spent most of my youth on fishing boats, where each day required physical toil. Yes, I was a rugged young man. It also had been three years since my maiden captain's voyage, and my strength was not what it once was. My hands were no longer callused from the sail rigging, nets, and oars. Of the women with us, Joanna held the most allure for me, though she could also be quite annoying.

Susanna watched Jesus, and like Joanna earlier, she sensed

trouble in the look he cast upon the men. She whispered to Joanna, who nodded in agreement. It sounded like they were worried about our eyes and ears. I later learned that Jesus was concerned that the men would never understand or be able to teach what he wanted us to know. He said we did not have eyes to see or ears to hear what he offered.

Before leaving the campfire later in the evening, Jesus said, "Joanna, before you prepare the evening meal, I would like you to share what you have learned about the eye of the needle and the Parable of Lack." Joanna had explained these stories before, but I had forgotten their meaning. I decided to stay and listen instead of following Jesus. The truth is, I stayed because I was quite hungry and just wanted to watch Joanna.

Joanna stood with her silhouette lit by the firelight and began. "Several months ago, Jesus told Magdalene, Susanna, Bathsheba, and me that we continued to lack one thing. At first, we were all very sad, and we really did not understand. Each of us felt that we had given all we could give and left behind all that we had known. Each of us desperately wanted to know that we were enough in Jesus's eyes. Jesus spent a great deal of time explaining what we lacked. He did this in his usual way, and he patiently waited for us to discover that each of his teachings had both an earthly and a divine message. We could then see and feel his saying, 'To give is to receive.' He prayed that we would have eyes to see, and all at once we each understood that giving up everything is how to receive the kingdom of God."

Susanna put the pot of stew over the fire as Joanna continued.

"We had many questions for Jesus, and he was patient with us. When we asked about some of his messages to the people who gathered by the olive tree, he added a little color. 'Blessed are the poor in spirit, for they have given away everything of this world, and theirs is the kingdom of heaven. Blessed are those who mourn and grieve what was once of value and vainly possessed, for they will be comforted. Blessed are the meek—those who humbly walk with one purpose, our Father's purpose—for they will inherit the earth'"[7]

Joanna ended by saying, "When Jesus expanded his parable with a little more detail, we each experienced a feeling of abundance, and we knew we lacked nothing. We could see that Jesus wanted our best, and our best involved giving up everything of this world that we clung to for safety and value. The worldly values and treasures were like evil spirits, diseases, and demons, and the desire for them left.[8] When I stopped valuing anything of this world, only then did I lack nothing."

Jesus came back to camp as Susanna started to pass out steaming bowls of food. We sat in silence, contemplating Joanna's words and enjoying the goat stew the women had prepared. Jesus then turned to Magdalene. "Tell the men the meaning of the Parable of Lack and the Parable of the Eye of the Needle," he said.

Magdalene was a beautiful woman, without flaw—the type of woman that inspires poems of love. Yet Magdalene felt she would never be enough for any man—that is, until she met Jesus that

---

[7] Matthew 5:3–5.

[8] Luke 8:2.

cold, rainy day, which felt to her like a lifetime ago. She had never married, but had known many men and felt a deep, irreparable flaw. She knew that she was truly loved the moment Jesus had said, "Follow me."

Magdalene smiled, grateful for the opportunity to please Jesus, saying, "My true heart's desire was realized as soon as I surrendered and gave up everything that had defined me, both the good and the bad. I have discovered the love I had been so desperately seeking where it could not be found. I only need to carry the mustard seed close to my heart."

When she finished speaking, Jesus smiled and said, "You have answered correctly."

Then Jesus looked at me and said, "Andrew, what possessions are you still holding onto?" Without waiting for a reply, he turned and walked off to pray by himself.

CHAPTER
FIVE

SUSANNA AND THE EYE OF THE NEEDLE

S usanna was another of the women who truly longed for an opportunity to help or serve Jesus. Every day, I saw her wake with a beautiful smile, lying on the open grass, no matter the night's cold or rain. Her servant's attitude surprised me to no end, given her royal bloodline. Susanna had rich long hair the color of the darkest coal, which she wore in a slave's braid. She was enthusiastic and verbose, with a beautiful innocence, as she had never known a man. Susanna gave up her vast earthly kingdom that she had inherited from the line of Solomon. Her holdings were so large that more than one lifetime was needed to visit its corners. She had many houses that she had never visited, and now, she never would. She had given all her possessions to her subjects and freed her many slaves. Several of the slaves followed her and supported her with the means she had provided to them for their freedom. My favorite of these was Bathsheba. Bathsheba would turn heads in every town and would someday be the downfall of kings. Her beauty caused me to stutter every time I tried to talk to her.

It was good to see the women and camp again. Jesus had sent me along with the other men to nearby villages a couple of days earlier, stating we should "find a house to put our peace upon." We each went as directed, but none of us were successful. No one fed us or welcomed us into their homes, and our travels back to camp seemed particularly dusty and long. Some of us made a brief stop in the small village of Carmel, which was along the east bank of the Jordan River. It made no sense to me to stay in town since none of us had any money. Jesus always sent us out without money, and we always came back the same way.

The evening camp was set by a quiet brook about a half hour's walk from the main city gates of Jerusalem. As the fire crackled and popped, and steam started to rise from the stew cauldron, I watched as Jesus went off to pray by himself. Then, Joanna went off to pray too. I started to think that perhaps I would try praying alone some evening, but not tonight. I later learned from Jesus that he left to pray before mealtime because the hunger pains always reminded him to connect to God. Hunger somehow made it easier for him.

Thankfully, and with a sigh of relief, I watched Susanna and Bathsheba hand out the evening meal of potatoes and goat stew. As Susanna was about to hand me my bowl, she asked if I would like to know what Jesus had taught her about his eye-of-the-needle parable during the past few days. I said that I would. But to my dismay, Susanna took my bowl of stew and went off to pray. When she returned to camp, she said to us twelve men, "Follow me to the well." Most of the others had finished their meals, but I had not yet started and was very hungry. The others rose, and I decided to follow Susanna on an empty stomach anyway. Perhaps I could get a drink at this well since I was also quite thirsty. As we walked, Susanna said that the well she spoke of was filled with the water Jesus offered. I did not understand and only knew that I was thirsty and hungry.

While we walked, Susanna began her lesson. "We have all heard Jesus tell the rich and the poor, the Romans and the Pharisees, the same thing: 'Go and sell everything you have, and you will find a treasure in heaven. Then, come and follow me.' He told each of them that they still lacked one thing, and over the past couple of years, you have witnessed many turn away from him in sadness and defeat. They were each fearful or perhaps defiant in their unwillingness to give up, leave, or sell certain possessions. Some possessions are obvious, such as money and clothes, but others are hidden. Do you remember what Jesus said to the young man who wanted to follow us after he buried his father? Even the poor could not leave everything behind and follow. 'With man, this is impossible, and with God all things are possible.'"[9] She paused for a moment and then spoke again. "Do you hear?" she asked.

My thoughts of food were fading, and I felt that I was starting to see what Susanna was trying to say. If I looked only to God, then it was possible and would be easy to leave everything else behind. I really didn't need anything but the peace of God. However, if I tried to give up everything else, including my desire to eat right at that moment, without God's strength, I would fail.

Peter said in frustration, "We have heard this all before, but what does it have to do with it being easier for a camel to go through the eye of a needle?"

Trying to support my brother, I chimed in and asked, "Where is the well?"

Susanna prayed again, to herself, and then she warned us with Jesus's words: "Not everyone will enter the kingdom of heaven, but only the ones who do the will of our Father.[10] So, make every effort to enter through the narrow door, because many will try to enter and will not be able to."[11] I thought I understood, but I could see that the others were as annoyed with her response as Peter and me. The men felt insulted but did not know what to do about it.

In her frustration, Susanna rapidly fired off questions to us. "Why is Jesus asking us to follow him and to take his yoke upon ourselves? What is he really talking about when he cries out,

---

[9] Matthew 19:27.

[10] Matthew 7:2.

[11] Luke 13:24.

'Indeed, it is easier for a camel to go through the eye of a needle than for someone who is rich to enter the kingdom of God?'"[12]

I shouted, "That's why we followed you to this well. And, by the way, there is no well here!" The men's confused looks were quickly changing into anger. Joanna and Bathsheba were nodding in agreement with Susanna and seemed at peace. They were clearly grateful for the extra time Jesus had spent explaining what they lacked.

Peter said, "Please, please, speak plainly and quickly. We do not like being taught by a woman who has nothing new to say. We know all of this! And where is this well you spoke of?"

By now, we were just outside of the walls of Jerusalem, and Susanna started to pray again, saying, "Father, help me say what you want me to say, and help them hear what you want them to hear."

It was an hour before midnight, and Susanna said, "Let us go into the city." The women had an understanding smile, but the men objected. We knew that the gates to the city closed at dusk.

"Why are we going into the city now?" I asked Peter. "The gates will be locked and guarded!"

"Let them go on, brother," Peter said, laughing. "We'll follow just to prove their foolishness!"

Approaching the city gate, Susanna and Bathsheba walked off the main road to the left side, down a well-worn dirt trail. There was a small, sturdy wooden door at the end of the path. The door was large enough to fit livestock through, provided the animal had

---

[12] Matthew 7:25.

no load. The narrow door allowed a man to walk through only if he bent his head down slightly. The entrance was easily defended and difficult to get through. Susanna knocked on the door, and the centurion on the other side answered. "Who desires to enter through the eye of the needle at this hour?"

Susanna replied, "My companions and I."

The centurion said, "Everyone must leave their weapons by the wall outside the door before entering the city."

Peter looked at me in amazement. "My eyes have been opened by a woman! It was obvious! A camel could pass through this small door only if it was stooped and its burden was removed. The camel cannot remove its own burden. I see myself for the first time in Jesus's parable. To enter the city of Jerusalem, I had only to give up my weapons and leave them behind. To enter through the door to the kingdom of God, I must give up all my worldly desires and my identity with them. Everything must go. Not letting everything go is what I lack." My brother seemed to be excited and at peace, but I still felt confused.

Susanna looked a bit proud. She could see that some of the men were finally beginning to see and understand. When I ducked to go through the door, she asked, "Can you see that Jesus has been trying to have you walk through the eye of the needle many times and in many ways? When he tells you to go and spread the good seed, but leave your purse, bag, and sandals behind. Can you see that he is asking you to leave everything but the mustard seed?[13] The mustard seed, the smallest of seeds, can easily fit through

---

[13] Luke 22:35.

the eye of a needle, yet it grows into a large tree like the word and faith of Jesus when it is firmly rooted in your heart. You continue to fail because you take your past with you through the narrow door. Leave your past where it belongs and only take hold of the mustard seed."

I could see Susanna glowing with excitement as she explained the meaning of walking through the eye-of-the-needle entrance in Jerusalem. I thought Jesus said he was planning to ride in through the city gates tomorrow or perhaps the day after. Some of the men, including me, were once again becoming frustrated and angry, and she stopped speaking. Bathsheba had taught Susanna that no men like being taught by a woman unless she is able to make them think it was their idea in the first place. This was an art that slaves were well versed in.

I felt that I might be getting the "lacked" idea, but I was still hungry and thirsty. I was not one who was upset easily, but I'd had enough. I turned to head back to camp alone with a parting shout, "There is no well, and the gates are closed. This is foolishness!"

Susanna calmly replied, "No one comes to the Father except through the eye of the needle! Our Father's word is the mustard seed, and the Kingdom of God awaits those with ears to hear and eyes to see. But many who are first will be last, and the last first!"[14]

I regretted saying anything and just kept walking.

---

[14] Matthew 7:31.

CHAPTER
SIX

BORN AGAIN

When I arrived at camp, only Jesus was sitting by the fire. He looked at my eyes in a soothing way. I was glassy-eyed and soon felt tears rolling down my cheeks. The impact of his gaze was ineffably calming. Jesus always seemed to know what I needed, especially when I didn't, and then he left.

I was sitting by the fire waiting for the others to return from the eye of the needle when I heard someone approach. I looked up to see a stranger dressed in the flowing robes of a religious leader. He was tall, a little round in the midsection, and clearly a Pharisee. He looked at me and demanded, "Do you know him?"

I was ready for the usual onslaught of typical questions: "Did he really walk on water? Did he turn water into wine—and, by the way, how was the wine?" and on and on. My standard reply for the past few months had been, "No, you have me mixed up with someone else. I have been told I look like the handsome rugged one, but I am not he."

Tonight, for some reason, I replied, "Yes, why do you ask?"

The Pharisee was none other than Nicodemus, a member of the Jewish Ruling Council. Without explanation, he begged, "I must see him!"

Nicodemus's fancy flowing clothes made me want to say, "Nice robe!" but I heard myself reply, "He's off praying and will return shortly." At least, I hoped he would return shortly.

As I turned to leave and look for Jesus, he walked into camp. "Greetings, Nicodemus," he said. "I have been waiting for you." I thought this should be an interesting conversation: the "fine-silk" man talks to the one with no shoes.

Nicodemus said, "I have come to you alone and at night, for reasons you know." He waited for Jesus to reply, but he didn't. Instead, Jesus just sat, looking at him. "We know that you are a teacher who has come from God, for no one could perform the signs you are doing if God were not with him."

I couldn't believe what I was hearing. The entire Jewish Ruling Council believed our Jesus has come from God Almighty!

Jesus replied to Nicodemus, "Very truly I tell you, no one can see the kingdom of God unless they are born again."

I shook my head and thought, "What in the world is he talking about now?"

Nicodemus was confused too and begged Jesus to understand. "How can someone be born when they are old?" he asked. "Surely they cannot enter a second time into their mother's womb to be born!"

Jesus answered, "Very truly I tell you, no one can enter the kingdom of God unless they are born of the Spirit. Flesh gives birth to flesh, but the Spirit gives birth to spirit. You should not be surprised to hear me say that you must be born again."

Some motion at the edge of camp caught my eye, and I glanced up in time to see the women stop as they approached the camp. Nicodemus bellowed, "How can this be?"

Jesus calmly replied, "You are Israel's teacher, but you do not understand these things. I have spoken to you of earthly things, and yet you do not believe. How then will you believe if I speak of heavenly things?" Nicodemus glared at Jesus and then stomped off into the night without another word.

His last words to Nicodemus were, "The wind blows wherever it pleases. You hear its sound, but you cannot tell where it comes from or where it is going. And so it is with everyone born of the Spirit."[15] Nicodemus's stride did not give any hint of whether or not he heard Jesus. I felt like shouting *let those with ears hear,* but thought that might be frowned upon.

Susanna came over to me and asked, "What just happened? Who was Jesus talking to by the fire?" I ignored her and turned away,

---

[15] John 3.

smiling to myself. I was glad I had left the women at Jerusalem's wall and returned to camp; I finally had knowledge of something that they knew nothing of!

I walked over to where the other men were now sitting and said, "You will never guess who came into camp!" At hearing this, Jesus stood up and left.

We gathered around the fire, and I told them of the fancy Pharisee, Nicodemus, who'd walked for hours just to seek Jesus's counsel. I told them that it seemed as though Jesus had been expecting him and about the odd conversation they'd had about being born again. I asked, "What do you think Jesus means by being born again?"

To my surprise, the men who had walked through the door of the eye of the needle sat me down for what they explained was "the much-needed conversation." Thomas decided to start. "The well that Susanna was leading us to was the same well that Jesus spoke of last week. Do you remember the Samaritan woman at the well? The water that always flowed, and once you drink of it, you will never be thirsty again." I nodded even though I was confused. "The water from that well is God's love," he said, "and once you drink, you will never thirst for anything else. You will be satisfied, and you will not be in lack. The eye of the needle is a metaphor to help you see that you cannot possess anything of this world if you want to enter the kingdom of God in this age. Just as the camel needs help removing its burden, so do you. Your burdens are your possessions, those that you have and those that you want. You cannot remove what you lack, and only with the water from this well will your possessions be of no interest to you. With man this is impossible, but with God, all things are possible."

My eyes were starting to glaze over, and my head pounded. Thomas's voice became even more convicted as he spoke. "To enter the kingdom of God, Andrew, you must give up everything except the one thing you lack. Our Father's word is like the mustard seed and easily fits through the eye of a needle. Other than this mustard seed, everything else must be abandoned—including your desire for possessions and any identity you have with them. You let these possessions create a false relationship within you that is of no value, and, in fact, separates you from the only one who is of value. That is what you lack. Do you understand?"

I heard them, but I couldn't understand. I got up and walked away, hoping my head would clear by the morning. I told them I was going off to pray. I lied.

CHAPTER
SEVEN

CHRYSALIS

The next morning was beautiful. I felt refreshed and only slightly confused. I decided that maybe the best thing to do was to sit alone and actually pray. I had not tried it before and had nothing to lose. As I found the perfect fallen tree trunk for the task at hand, Joanna and Susanna found me. They had brought some bread and asked if they might sit with me. With resignation, I replied, "Do I have a choice?"

Joanna took my hand and looked into my eyes for a moment. Then she closed her eyes and prayed. She whispered to God, "Give me your words and any sign that might help me reach Andrew." As she opened her eyes, she smiled and looked at me with hope. "Do you see that furry striped caterpillar eating a green leaf? The eye of the needle is like the chrysalis."

What started as a beautiful day was turning into another morning headache, and I was suddenly not feeling so refreshed.

Joanna continued, "The caterpillar leaves all he knows, all of the familiar patterns of his life—what he eats and what he wears are all left behind when he enters through his narrow door, his cocoon. To the caterpillar, this decision looks like and feels like death, and in a way, it is a death that must occur. Do you see, Andrew? After the transformation, he will no longer be called a caterpillar. This is like your brother, Peter, sometimes being called Simon."

My head was officially pounding. I never understood why Jesus called my brother different names at different times. I was glad that everyone always just called me Andrew. Although, come to think of it, my family used to call me "Hey."

Joanna went on. "Our Father sees rebirth for the caterpillar, not death. This happens by a renewing of the caterpillar's mind and a transformation of its life. The caterpillar's food is of no interest to the butterfly, and the butterfly is no longer constrained. This is all on display for the world to see what God has done. The butterfly, like the lamp on a hill, must not be hidden from others or from itself. When you get rid of all your possessions to go through the eye of the needle, you also will be able to fly. Do you hear, Andrew?"

I replied, "Of course I can hear. You are sitting inches from me."

To add to my frustration, Susanna meekly offered, "Going through the eye of the needle and emerging as a new creation is how we are born again. Last night, Nicodemus was not yet ready to see why Jesus said that we must be born again. The butterfly leaves its caterpillar desires, thoughts, and ways behind. In this way, so must you leave your worldly desires, thoughts, and ways. Just as the butterfly takes flight with only the concerns of its renewed and transformed mind and life, you must take flight with only concerns of the spirit. The caterpillar cannot see or imagine a life in flight, in freedom, or without lack, and so it is with us. Do you see why Jesus says that this is only possible with God? Do you hear?"

"Thank you. Yes, I see and hear now," I lied. "Let us pray in silence together." I did not mean this, of course; I just wanted them to stop talking. Thank God it worked!

Joanna and Susanna were pleased with my reply and sat quietly on either side of me. I drifted into thought about a conversation I'd had with Jesus the year before, when he said, "As you await the birth of a child from your wife's womb, so you await your birth from this body and mind." I wondered if this somehow related to the caterpillar or walking through the eye of the needle.

I then thought about Jesus calling my brother by different names. When he met Peter by the shore's edge, he had simply said, "Follow me," and we did. We did not know why, but we left all we knew behind. He told Peter, "Follow, leave purse, bag, and sandals, and you will not lack."[16] I remembered my brother saying how full he'd felt that day, with an abundance he had never known. That was when Jesus first started calling him Simon.

I felt puzzled, and my headache wasn't helping. I thought about

---

[16] Luke 22:35.

Jesus calling my brother Simon Peter, Simon, and Peter—all three names, and all just yesterday. "Is Peter in the cocoon?" I wondered. "Is it time for me to stop eating green leaves? Not yet," I thought. I opened my eyes when I smelled warm bread and a goat-stew dinner. The women were gone. I had been sitting there all day.

CHAPTER
EIGHT

POVERTY

The following morning was as good as it gets when traveling with Jesus. The women had a fire going, and the scent of baking bread filled the air. Jesus had gone to pray an hour before sunrise. Everyone in our camp had finished eating by the time he returned. He sat among us, warming himself. Magdalene brought Jesus a plate of food, and he ate. Jesus continued to practice silence and solitude with more frequency, and some of us wondered if he did not like our company.

I thought of myself as the quiet one, but I guess I was not really so quiet. I asked Jesus, "Did you really say that John the Baptist is greater than you and that, among those born of a woman, there is no one greater than John?"[17] I knew that John was more than a prophet and that he had baptized many in the tributaries to the Tigris River, including Jesus.

Jesus did not respond or look up; he simply finished his meal and went off to pray again.

The women smiled and seemed to understand my confusion, as did Thomas, apparently. Several people chuckled as Thomas pulled out his parchment notes and said, "Andrew, you are partly correct. Jesus said, 'Among those born of women, from Adam until John the Baptist, there is no one so superior to John the Baptist that his eyes should not be lowered before him.'"[18] Thomas was the tallest follower of Jesus, and we thought he was wise beyond his years and very dependable. He was close in age to my brother, Peter, and, before becoming a blacksmith, had spent most of his life in study in the capital city of Rome.

Thomas went on. "Do you see that both statements are correct, since Jesus was born after John?" I tried to let that sink in, but I still didn't really understand.

The rest of the morning was uneventful. When Jesus returned to camp, he said the phrase we were all familiar with: "Follow me." I wondered why he kept saying it. Who else would we follow? Certainly not Susanna; she would take everyone to an imaginary well or to a city after the gates were closed. There was to be a lot of walking this morning, and it was hot and dry long after midday. I had not seen a cloud for a few days.

---

[17] Luke 7:28.

[18] Thomas 46.

I found myself in an occasional trance watching the women walk, especially Bathsheba. Not many young girls are named *Bathsheba* these days. She had the most striking full features of any woman I had ever seen. She was very kind and openly grateful to Susanna for her freedom, and also for the purse Susanna had given her. Bathsheba was like a lily of the valley in sight and smell. I knew that many poems would be born because of her beauty and that she would likely ruin a king or two.

I snapped out of my daydream and looked at Jesus. "Teacher, did you say something like, 'the kingdom of God is within you?'"[19] I felt like Jesus had said something else, too, but I could not remember and thought it had to do with why I had no money. Jesus smiled at me, but then he walked off to pray. "There he goes again," I thought, shaking my head.

The women looked at me with pity. Joanna said, "I'm sorry, Andrew, but I can't recall exactly what Jesus said either!"

Dependable Thomas unrolled his parchment with great care and read, "Andrew, the kingdom of God is inside of you and outside of you. When you come to know yourself, then you will become known, and you will realize that it is you who are a son of the living Father. But if you will not know yourself, you will dwell in poverty—and it is you, Andrew, who are the poverty.[20] Do you hear? The more you know yourself, the more you will know God. The more you know God, the more you will know yourself." I felt

---

[19] Luke 17:21.

[20] Thomas 3.

another headache coming on, but I kept walking. I was grateful to have the sway of Bathsheba's hips in front of me.

No one said anything when Jesus returned. I felt a tension after Thomas read from the scroll, as I wondered if we were in poverty—or worse, if we *were* the poverty! Even more concerning, was I that poverty? I thought it must have had to do with a lack of money, and I wondered why Jesus kept telling us that we lacked one thing. Was that lack what causes me to dwell in poverty? Did this have something to do with the idea that "the poor will have the kingdom of heaven" or that "the meek will inherit the earth"? I remembered Thomas making note of this last month when we were sitting by a mountainside, surrounded by the large crowd from Corinth. I would try to remember to ask Thomas about it after the evening meal. I was exhausted just thinking about whether or not I was the poverty.

After a short break, Jesus stood again and said, "Follow me."

"He sure likes to say that," I thought. As Jesus and I walked, I began to wonder what those two words really meant. I was wondering a lot of things lately.

CHAPTER

NINE

MY MOTHER, MY BROTHER, MY SISTER

W e walked for a short distance until Jesus stopped unexpectedly and said, "We will spend the night here."

I thought, *What was wrong with the olive tree that was only a half mile back and had water and shelter?* I could never understand what Jesus was doing or why; none of it made any sense. I was just as likely to find the answer blowing in the wind as I was to find it from Jesus. Then I remembered his words to Nicodemus: "The wind blows wherever it pleases. You hear its sound, but you cannot tell where it

comes from or where it is going, and so it is with everyone reborn."
I sat by myself, thinking about how each of his teachings started
to fit together, like pieces of a puzzle.

We camped near a small trailhead. The fire was beginning to
die down, and I was nodding in and out of sleep. Suddenly, a young
boy of about thirteen appeared, shouting, "Is he here? Am I in the
right camp? He is my brother!" The boy was so excited and had
hope beaming from his eyes. He looked like he had not eaten or
slept in days, and his smell was worse than that of a goat herder.
I couldn't believe it—first, finely dressed and well-fed Nicodemus
showed up looking for Jesus and now this young, half-starved
beggar. Joanna gave him some stew, and he quieted down.

The others seemed to understand the boy's excitement. Peter
asked me if I remembered what had been said just yesterday in
the village we'd passed. Jesus had stopped for only a few minutes,
talking to Martha and Magdalene in their farmhouse, when
someone outside shouted, "Your mother and brothers are outside
and want to see you. They have news of your father!"

Jesus asked, "Who is my mother, and who are my brothers?"
He pointed to the twelve men and the four women with us saying,
"Here are my mother and my brothers, for whoever does the will
of our Father is my brother and my sister and my mother."[21] He
smiled gratefully at Joanna, Susanna, Bathsheba, and Magdalene.

To me, Jesus's reply seemed harsh—just like the reply he gave
last week when a woman shouted out with joy, "Blessed is the
mother who gave you birth and who nursed you." I thought Jesus

---

[21] Matthew 12:46–50.

would be happy with that, as we all nodded and were grateful for his mother bringing our teacher into this world. I had gained so much wisdom over the past three years—or so I thought until I heard his reply. "Blessed rather are those who hear the word of God and obey it."[22]

I had wanted to shout, "Jesus, can't you just smile and say thank you? Do you always have to be so direct and state how you really feel? How about letting the poor woman have her moment?"

Come to think of it, when Jesus was around the Jewish rulers, he often looked them in the eye and said, "My mother and brothers are those who hear God's word and put it into practice," and then he would turn his back on them and walk off.[23] Jesus told me he was trying to help the Pharisees see that they do not practice God's Word. They only tell others to follow the Torah. It reminded me of one of my father's sayings, "Do as I say, not as I do." Jesus seemed to have little use for religious leaders of any kind.

I continued to daydream about his "mother-brother" response. Questions flowed in my mind with no obvious answer: was my duty to our Father in heaven or to the people he placed in my care? Did I answer only to my Father in heaven or also to my family in Naphtali? Why did my brother, Peter, follow someone who had given up everything and encouraged others to do the same? It made no sense. The sounds of dinner let me put these questions and thoughts away for another day.

---

[22] Luke 11:27–28.
[23] Luke 8:21.

I was enjoying silent prayer after our meal, when the shouts and sounds of the boy's voice pierced my ears again. "Is my brother here? Please tell me. Please!"

I kept to my prayers, but his pleases continued. "Yes, your brother is here," I finally answered. "Now please be quiet. He is off praying, as I am."

The boy calmed down, and said, "Thank you. My name is James."

Early the next morning, I awoke to see the fire going strong. As usual, the air smelled of baking bread. I relaxed with my thoughts and watched James sleeping soundly. The fire popped and little James sat up suddenly. He looked around to find his big brother, but his face fell when he didn't see him in the camp. He pleaded with Susanna, "Where is he? I have news of our father!"

I tossed, and then turned over and mumbled, "He's probably off praying again."

Jesus appeared and James ran to his side, leaving Susanna sitting alone by the fire. Jesus then turned to me and said, "Wash Susanna's feet," before leaving with James. I was hoping he was talking to someone else, but looking around, I quickly discovered that no one else was in camp.

There was no way I was about to wash Susanna's feet. I was still angry with her about the trick she'd played on us by taking us to a well that wasn't there and then walking to the city gates after they were closed. It also confounded me that Susanna and the other women understood Jesus's parables far better than any of the men—except Thomas. Under my breath I said, "Not a chance."

Somehow, though, I found myself bringing water, oil, and a cloth to where Susanna was seated—almost as if it were someone else's hands doing the work.

Susanna and I did not speak or look at each other. I picked up her left foot and felt a little uneasy as I untied her sandal's laces. Holding Susanna's foot in my palm, I dipped the cloth in the water and gently began to wipe the soil away from her skin. As I worked, I noticed how delicate her foot was—and also how bruised. In fact, her foot was covered in small, fresh cuts. As I applied the oil, I wondered how her feet had come to be this way. And why was the blood fresh?

It was shortly after daybreak as I slid her sandal back into place and snuggly tied the laces, taking care to be as gentle as possible with her injuries.

Not a word had passed between us. Still feeling uneasy, I took her right foot in my hand and repeated the process. For the first time that morning, I noticed the warmth of the fire on my back and the basket at Susanna's side. I suddenly realized that she must have arisen hours before daybreak and walked into the night to bring fresh bread to our camp. There were thorn bushes along the path that could not be seen with a new moon, like the one we'd had the night before. Was Susanna the one who had started the fire that morning? I had taken for granted that someone always did, but I had never stopped to think it might be Susanna.

I finished cleaning and applying oil to Susanna's foot, and an unfamiliar emotion emerged from within me. A tear rolled down my cheek and fell on her foot. "I am sorry," I said, looking up at her.

A second later, Jesus and James showed up. I still felt uneasy but also forgiven and blessed. Only a short time before, I had sworn that I would never clean Susanna's bare feet. But now? I did not understand what had happened, and I recalled my brother objecting to Jesus washing his feet—which was something Jesus did for each of us regularly.[24] I never understood why he did that. I settled back into my sleeping position and drifted off, dreaming of the time I first remembered Jesus washing our feet.

When Jesus had come to Peter with a cloth and water, my brother said, "Why are you going to wash my feet?"

Jesus replied, "You do not realize now what I am doing, but later you will understand."

"No," said Peter, "you shall never wash my feet."

Jesus answered, "Unless I wash you, you have no part with me."

Peter replied, "Then not just my feet, but my hands and my head as well!"

Jesus answered, "Those whose feet have been washed, their whole body is cleansed. And you are clean, though not every one of you. The one that is not clean will betray me."

When he had finished washing our feet, Jesus put on his clothes and returned to his place by the fire. "Do you understand what I have done for you?" he asked us. "You call me *teacher*, and rightly so, for that is what I am. Now that I have washed your feet, you also should wash one another's feet. I have set you an example that you should do as I have done for you. Very truly I tell you, no servant is greater than his master, nor is a messenger greater than the one

---

[24] John 13:6.

who sent him. Now that you know these things, you will be blessed if you do them."

Jesus had washed my feet, and now I'd washed Susanna's. Was I supposed to do as Jesus did? In everything? Was that what he was showing me? If it meant that I was supposed to give up everything, I knew I wasn't ready.

"Is this boy, James, your brother—or your actual brother?" I asked Jesus. "Oh, you know what I am trying to say." James took some fresh bread from Susanna's basket and smiled. Then he grasped his big brother's hand, and they walked off again without a word.

Jesus never answered my question and seemed to walk off every time I asked anything these days, so it was no surprise when it happened this time. Yet, every time this occurred, there always seemed to be an unexpected discovery of what I sought. I knew that I needed to break down the wall of unforgiveness I had toward Susanna, and I also knew that my pride was standing in the way. This morning, I felt forgiveness that I'd never asked for. As others joined the morning meal, I stared at the fire and drifted into thought.

Jesus had said that forgiveness was for the person doing the forgiving. What did he mean? I asked some questions about this at breakfast. Thomas pulled out a parchment and said, "Your heavenly Father will forgive you if you forgive all people when they sin against you. But if you do not forgive others of their sins, your Father will not forgive your sins."[25] This last part got my attention.

---

[25] Matthew 6:14–15.

Thomas went on. "Jesus also said, 'Forgive us our debts, as we also have forgiven our debtors.'"[26]

This seemed like odd wording to me; it meant that I had already forgiven and that I had been forgiven, as if the offense was in the past. Then it dawned on me: the offense was always in the past. This made some sense, but I still wasn't sure. "Didn't someone say that our Father blots out our wrongs and our sins are remembered no more, or something like that?" I mumbled.

Thomas replied, "In a conversation God had with the Prophet Isaiah, God said, 'I, even I, am he who blots out all of your transgressions for my own sake.'"[27]

I was still confused. Was I supposed to blot out what others did wrong for my own sake or for theirs? This was another area that eluded me for the moment. I did not have ears to hear or eyes to see, but I felt sure that I had experienced something wonderful with Susanna that morning. There was compassion and forgiveness between us, yet I had no understanding of the means. I was starting to wonder if Jesus knew that this would happen. He always seemed to leave and return at just the right moment.

---

[26] Luke 11:2–4.
[27] Isaiah 43:25.

CHAPTER

TEN

OUR FATHER

L ater that day, I watched Jesus and young James as they sat and talked together. James kept looking up at the brother he'd heard so much about, almost as if he were afraid to speak. He had seemed anxious to say something for two days now, but each time he was about to do so, he was told to just listen. As they sat enjoying the moment together, Jesus asked, "What news do you bring from Nazareth?"

A sadness came over James's face, and he cast his eyes to the ground. "Our father has been killed," he uttered.

Jesus was silent. He clearly loved his little brother, gazing at him as James started to speak again, nervously. "After you left,

Father spoke of you all the time. He often told of God talking to him about you before you were born. He wasn't positive it was God's voice, but he said it sure sounded like God! He said that you were a Nazirite, dedicated to God while you were still in mom's womb. Are you a Nazirite, brother? Father said he trusted the voice and was rewarded with you as his son to care for, even if only for a short time. He was always thanking God for guidance—and for you."

"Father told me about one winter night when he was sleeping soundly and abruptly woke from a dream, a dreadful dream. In the dream, he was instructed to get up immediately and take you to a foreign land. The ruler of our homeland, Herod, was searching for you and planned to kill you! Mom questioned his dream, but they left on a long journey to the other side of the Tigris. Father told me that they had to leave everything they knew—friends, family, our house, food, fields, and work."

I thought to myself, "Jesus's family left everything and followed God." Wasn't this what Jesus was doing when he sent us to find a house to put our peace upon in a foreign town and without any money or food?

James continued, "In the dream God said they could not come back until Herod's death.[28] Father, too, had doubts as the journey grew long and there was little food or shelter. They could not even tell anyone where they were from or where they were going for fear of Herod's spies."

"Mother heard news one day of Herod's death order and was overcome with grief. 'The dream was true!' she cried, and she was

---

[28] Matthew 2.

more fearful than ever. Did you know that Herod ordered all the young boys in Bethlehem and the surrounding towns and villages to be sacrificed?" James paused for a moment to look at Jesus. Then he said, "Is sacrificed a pleasant way of saying slaughtered? No one had ever seen or heard or imagined such wasted life and innocent blood spilled before or since, and Mother told me of the great wailing and sorrow felt in every town."

Jesus did not say anything and listened as James continued. "After Herod's death, Father was still fearful, so he did not go back to our home. Instead, he chose a small town in Galilee called Nazareth. Did you know that everyone from that town refers to you as the Nazarene? Sounds like *Nazirite* to me. What do you think, brother? Have you heard all this before? Do you think God talked to our father about you?"

Thomas and I had been listening to James from a distance and felt empathy for him. Thomas made notes on parchment to discuss later; parchment and pen were his constant companion.

Jesus's response to James was unsettling. "James, from this moment forward, do not call anyone on earth 'father,' for you have one Father, and he is in heaven."[29]

Jesus put his arm around James. James nodded to his big brother, and they were silent for a time. James's eyes lit up suddenly, and he said, "Father's other favorite story was when you snuck off when you were just twelve years old! Mother asked if you were with us, and Father said yes. He lied! Oh, sorry. I said *father* twice."

Without pausing for air, James's words just flowed. "This story

---

[29] Matthew 6:14.

took place in a time before I was born, so I liked hearing about you. We always went to the annual festival in Jerusalem. I think it's so our parents could recount stories about you. He knew you had left in the night, where you were going, and why, as God had come to him in a dream again. Sorry, I meant to say, our Father had come to him in a dream. In the dream, he explained what he must do, and to let you go. Our Father assured him that you would be fine and that you would be found in the temple, listening and teaching. For a whole day, Dad lied to Mom, telling her that he had just seen you, and not to worry—you know how she is—and finally he admitted that you were back in Jerusalem. Mother always interrupted him at this point in the story with great panic in her voice. 'It took three days to find my son!' she would say. Then she would tell of when she saw you and yelled, 'Son, why have you treated us like this? Your father and I have been anxiously searching for you.'[30] You were a year younger than I am now, and your reply did not make Mom very happy. Do you remember what you said?"

Jesus looked down and smiled tenderly. "Yes, I do. 'Why were you searching for me? Didn't you know I had to be in my Father's house?' James, do you see why I say you have one Father who is in heaven, and he is always with you and watching out for you? He is watching out for me and for each of us."

"I'm not sure," James replied. "I know our parents said they did not understand what you were saying! But secretly, Dad pulled me aside and said he was very pleased with you. He was proud of you, and he loved you."

---

[30] Luke 2:42–52.

Thomas and I had been jotting down the conversation. When Jesus noticed us, he left to pray by himself. We joined James and were happy to have time to ask him about the details of Jesus's early days. I told James, "I almost always spend some part of the day wondering what your brother is really saying. He has given us so many lessons in parables. Several of us try to write them down and, when time permits, compare notes. When we give your brother a puzzled look, he usually asks us to examine who we see ourselves as in his parables and search for the meaning in that identity."

"What is a parable?" James asked. I told James he would find out shortly, but that they usually end with, "Whoever has ears to hear, let them hear, or whoever has eyes to see, let them see."

James' eyes went wide. "That's how I ended up here! I was in school, reading from the story of Jonah, and I blurted out those exact words: 'whoever has ears to hear, let them hear.' My teacher became very mad and told me to leave the class. Instead of going home, however, I came searching for my brother."

Jesus returned just as Thomas asked James, "No one knows you are here? Not your parents, not anyone?"

Jesus looked at James and said, "Follow me." Those two words usually meant something, and I didn't think we would ever see young James again. When they left, I followed them at a distance to see if there would be an opportunity to hug James and send him off with a little bread and water.

CHAPTER
ELEVEN

BROTHER JAMES

I watched the two brothers walk and then sit down in the open field. This was the same field where the buck had once snorted and woke me. No words passed between them, and Jesus closed his eyes. James seemed familiar with this practice, and he did the same.

When they did finally opened their eyes, Jesus turned to young James and said, "You must listen and then go back to Mom. My words are a trial for you, and you will face many kinds. Consider these trials joy. Even though they do not feel like joy, consider them such. It is in the testing of your faith that perseverance is produced in you. Only a trial can help you with truly trusting our Father. Do not conform to the patterns of this world, and let perseverance finish her work in you, James. Even though you are just thirteen, perseverance will deliver you to maturity before your fourteenth year. You will be complete, not lacking anything.[31] Only a few of my followers understand when I say, 'You lack one thing.' Once you walk through trials with God, you will not lack. Abundance awaits you in this life, James."

Jesus then referenced the story of Jonah. "For the sun rises with scorching heat and withers the plant; its blossom falls, and its beauty is destroyed. Jonah did not understand this when our Father grew the plant and then produced the worm to eat the plant. Jonah did not understand even the smallest trial and remained a victim. In the same way, the rich will fade away even while they go about their business.[32] Do you see?"

James looked puzzled, but Jesus continued. "Do not desire the things valued by the world, as they are detestable in our Father's eyes. Those who do are always dragged away by their own evil desire and enticed.[33] When you do not conform to the patterns of others, you will lack nothing and will gain the crown of life. You will experience the treasures of heaven here on earth and in this age. Susanna does not lack."

They sat in silence for a while and held hands. Then Jesus said to James, "Be quick to listen, slow to speak, and slow to anger, but do not merely listen to our Father's word, and so deceive yourself,

---

[31] James 1:2–4.

[32] James 1:11.

[33] James 1:15.

but do what it says.[34] Also, unless you fast to the world, you shall not find abundance in the kingdom."[35] Jesus's voice trailed off as their time together was drawing to a close.

James wanted to remain with his brother. "Everyone calls you *Teacher*. Are you religious?" he asked.

Jesus replied, "For most, their religion is worthless. Their actions demonstrate that their words are of little or no value. 'Do as I say, not as I do.' Most are hypocrites. The religion that God our Father accepts is to look after orphans and widows and to keep oneself from being polluted by the world.[36] We have little time, so I will explain. All of my parables have interpretations that most people are not ready to see. Orphans and widows are those who are separated from accepting the love of our Father—from accepting that they are loved and cared for by the creator of everything. As you accept our Father's love, then you will be able to give love. If you seek any good from this world, you will lack and be in poverty. There is only one who is good, and you are to seek only him."

They sat in silence for a few more moments, but then Jesus stood saying, "I must take the cup our Father handed me," and he turned to walk back to camp. James sat for a while and reflected on how his brother tried to tell him the same message in many ways. I went to sit with James, and he said, "I am going to take the cup my brother just handed me and start walking toward Galilee." I did not see a cup and did not understand what James was saying, which

---

[34] James 1:19.

[35] Second Logion.

[36] James 1:26–27.

was not unusual for me. He would be fourteen in a month, and he would follow his brother's instructions. I thought, *Little James must have wondered what trial would be coming that month that would bring him to maturity.* I was certainly wondering myself.

CHAPTER

TWELVE

THE FARMER
AND HIS WEEDS

J esus did not return the next day, which was not unusual. Once,
he had been gone for forty days with no word or explanation.
Several of us sat under an olive tree, discussing the parchment
notes from the previous week when Jesus taught to the large crowd
by the western shore of the Sea of Galilee. Thomas was reading
from the Parable of the Farmer and I smiled, recalling the morning
we'd first met Jesus when he'd told Peter he would become a sower
of men—or was it a fisher of men?

Thomas read his notes aloud. "As the farmer scattered seed,

some fell along the path and the birds ate it, some fell on rocky places with little soil, and it sprang up quickly and withered because it had no root."[37]

I said, "Because it had no moisture."

Thomas did not like being corrected, so he ignored my comment and continued. "Other seed fell among thorns, which grew up and choked the plants."

I jumped in again and said, "So that they did not bear grain."[38]

I could see that Thomas was getting annoyed, but he continued. "Still, other seed fell on good soil, where it produced a crop a hundred times what was sown."

I couldn't help smiling and interrupted again. "Then Jesus shouted, 'Whoever has ears, let them hear.[39] Can you see yourself in the parable? Are you the bad seed, poor soil, or farmer sowing?" I surprised myself by asking this.

Just then, Susanna and Joanna arrived, and I rose to greet them. The others were glad that I was getting along better with Susanna, and I was sure they probably wondered what had happened to change the temperature between us. Joanna handed out some bread and figs, and Susanna brought us a vase of water. As I watched them work, I marveled at how they could sway so wonderfully and balance a load on their heads.

The water and meal were welcomed by us all. Afterward, we continued to go over the parchment and Jesus's explanation of

---

[37] Luke 8:6.

[38] Mark 4:7.

[39] Luke 8:8.

the Parable of the Farmer. We sat in silence for a time, each of us wondered what type of soil we really were. In truth, I'm sure that we were far more concerned about the type of soil others thought we were, and especially about how Jesus viewed us.

I finally broke the silence, saying that I thought I might be the soil along the path, as I never really seemed to hear or see what Jesus was saying. I hoped that someone would disagree, but I saw only nodding heads. I realized that the only time I had experienced any real fruit was when I obeyed and washed Susanna's feet.

Peter spoke next. "I'm a little further along than my younger brother, but I'm also very concerned. I cannot believe that I might be the rocky ground, receiving the word quickly and with joy."

My brother had told me that he always felt full of conviction and strong in the moment while in Jesus's presence, but he has been troubled ever since Jesus told him that he had no root. Jesus said that when trouble came, Peter would deny that he even knew Jesus or any of us or even me, his own flesh and blood! Jesus told him that when the test came, Peter would deny him three times, to three different people.

"How can this be possible?" Peter asked me. "I would go to prison or die for him! It's not true. I can't be rocky soil." I wondered if Peter would recall these words when the time came.

I was deep in thought about being poverty, poor soil, and someone who lacked, and I blurted out, "Earlier, I asked Jesus what he meant when he said, 'The first will be last and the last will be first.' I thought he was going to walk away as he usually did when

I asked this question, but instead, Jesus turned and said, 'You will understand tomorrow.' Why would he say that?"

Joanna, Susanna, and Magdalene looked at each other, and tears welled in their eyes. I later learned that they knew Jesus's time to leave us was near. I know now the sense of urgency they felt, and that they wished Jesus had spent more time with the men. Susanna said that he felt we were his greatest failure. But how could he have spent more time with us? He spent twenty-four hours with us every day for three years!

Joanna could no longer contain her thoughts. "Do you not understand his parable? The soil lacks because it contains things of this world, and the soil is you. Do you not remember the Parable of Lack, or the Parable of the Eye of the Needle? This is no different. The rocky soil requires each rock be removed. This is impossible for man, as man cannot remove his own rocks—just as the camel had to lose its load before passing through the eye of the needle narrow doorway. The soil with thorns and weeds must have these removed before it can be productive. Again, with man, this is impossible." She paused. "What you lack is that you have desires for things other than God.

"With the farmer, who is our Father, all things are possible. The soil contains thorns, weeds, and rocks, and these represent the patterns and desires of this world—things that are in each of us and are falsely valued in our own eyes, and detestable in God's sight. The cost to enter the kingdom of God and to be good soil is to give up everything—all the weeds and thorns—and then follow. In this parable, *everything* includes desire, the worries of life, the deceitfulness of wealth, and the pleasures that choke like the weeds. All must be thrown into the fire. Otherwise, the soil—you—will be unfruitful, immature, and lacking."[40] Joanna glanced at each of us, saw that we were still struggling, and looked to Susanna and Magdalene for help.

Susanna added, "The lack is in false relationships that are of no real value. Is your relationship with money of any real value? What you have is what you lack. Do you see that tending to the soil is only possible with God? It is impossible with the world, with the weeds that choke out God's green pasture. Thorns and rocks show up as worry, judgment, guilt, gossip, condemnation, unforgiveness, selfishness, greed, malice, deceit, lewdness, envy, slander, arrogance, and folly."[41]

I wanted to shout, "Slow down, Miss High Horse!" Jesus had once said to enter through the narrow door before it closed. Was the narrow door closing—or worse, had it already closed?

Magdalene said, "A weed is fear of those who can kill the body."[42] Magdalene tried to encourage us and recalled the words from Thomas's parchment. "You will not lack when you truly know who you are, and then you will know that you are each the son of the living Father. Our father has no grandchildren! Do you see? If you will not know yourselves, you will dwell in poverty, and it is you who are that poverty.[43] You will be rocky soil or the path, or soil

---

[40] Matthew 13:22.

[41] Mark 7:22.

[42] Matthew 10:28.

[43] Thomas 3.

choked out by weeds, and then, in short, you will lack and be the poverty!" Magdalene paused and sighed. Then she said, "Perhaps we should go back to the eye of the needle tonight to discuss this further."

Thomas said, "Remember, we had to take off all our armor to enter through the eye of the needle narrow door of the city. The armor is the same as the weeds and rocks. The armor is the things of this world that we value more than God." I instinctively knew that Thomas and the women were right, but I just could not see it clearly. I certainly could not help the others see.

Jesus appeared and said, "Children, you are not of this world any more than I am of this world."[44] Then he was gone again.

I shook my head and walked off, mumbling, "I am not of this world? Really?" I had decided that I might not ever understand. The others carefully rolled their scrolls, tucked them under their arms, and continued along the road until sunset.

---

[44] John 17:16.

THIRTEEN

THE PHARISEE'S FEAR

It started out as just another ordinary day, the usual smells of the campfire and baking bread filling the air as we awoke. The day was hot and dusty, and the wind changed direction several times. I kept moving around the fire to avoid the smoke. The morning was uneventful, but the women were unusually quiet. A donkey showed up as if on cue, and Jesus hopped onto it. "Follow me," he said.

I was thinking, "Clearly we all lacked, as no one had any possessions, except for a few of Susanna's slaves." With no packing needed, we were walking toward the city within minutes, and I felt that I would understand soon—although it was apparently not yet my time. Would I ever see myself as my Father saw me? Would I ever see myself as the farmer? I was very thankful for Bathsheba, Susanna, and Joanna for their insight and encouragement, as well as their cooking, fire-tending, and swaying.

When we entered Jerusalem, with Jesus riding on the donkey, the whole city was stirred. "Who is this?" people asked. The crowds were bigger than any of us had ever seen or imagined. Justus, one of Jesus's childhood friends, shouted, "He is from Nazareth in Galilee."[45] Justus was hoping to impress others by association, but it only annoyed me.

I recognized Nicodemus and read a worried look on his face as Susanna and Bathsheba walked by him and the other members of the Jewish ruling council. Susanna was trying to discern any possible trouble for Jesus that might be avoided. One of the Pharisees said to his friend, "See, this is getting us nowhere. Look how the whole world has gone after him!"[46]

A calmness seemed to settle over the women, as if they realized that the time was now and that Jesus would soon drink from his cup. He lacked nothing and did not fear losing it all. I think they understood that Jesus would willingly lose his life for any of us, but they did not know how to explain this to the men. I saw a look of hope flash across Joanna's face when Judas made his way over to the Pharisees. Jesus spent more time with Judas than any of the

---

[45] Matthew 21:11.

[46] John 12:19.

other men, and he genuinely seemed to encourage and take the extra time to explain his parables to him. Judas told me on more than one occasion that Jesus liked him best. Perhaps Judas could help, as he seemed to know the Pharisees too.

FOURTEEN

AN UNEXPECTED SCATTERING

It had been a truly glorious day, and the camp was abuzz with excitement. The other men and I thought that our hard work of going to towns and villages, proclaiming the good news, had all been worth the effort. The hour Jesus had spoken of was now, and surely all the people would become good soil and receive the kingdom! It was so exhilarating, but yet blissfully exhausting. I knew we would sleep well tonight. As the fire died down, I went to find Jesus. I wanted to ask him a question, but before I could get it out, he said, "Sit here while I pray." He walked a short distance away from camp. I called Peter and Thomas over to help me stay awake; after all, Jesus might be praying for forty days! Our eyes were heavy, as it had been a truly long day.[47]

Jesus returned later that night as Peter and I were sleeping soundly. I woke when I heard Jesus say, "Simon, watch and pray so that you will not fall into temptation. The flesh is weak."[48] Now he was calling my brother Simon and not Peter—the two-name thing was confounding! I rolled over and returned to undisturbed sleep, drifting into dreams of the difference between a caterpillar and a butterfly. They were the same creature but called by different names.

Eventually, a wet log popped loudly on the fire and woke me. I sat up to see Joanna watching Jesus from behind a nearby tree. The campfire lit her face, and tears rolled down her cheeks. She could see that her beloved was deeply distressed and troubled. As the rest of our camp slept soundly, I knew Joanna mourned for Jesus's grief over our failures and viewed them as his own. She watched as Jesus looked to heaven and said, "My soul is overwhelmed with sorrow to the point of death." He clearly felt he had failed those whom God had placed in his care. Jesus whispered, "Father, what will it take for them to see? Must I give it all?" He turned a little further from camp and fell to the ground. Joanna continued to weep as she heard Jesus's agonizing prayers, crying out to his Father, and her heart was broken.

Then, out of the darkness and without warning, centurions

---

[47] Matthew 26:43.

[48] Matthew 26:41.

appeared in full battle dress. With arms drawn, they surrounded the camp. They encircled Jesus and seized him, and my brother and I ran from our camp. We heard the cries of the other men as they fearfully scattered into the night.

The women were stunned, suddenly alone and weeping in despair. They wailed over Jesus's arrest, and I heard Joanna cry, "Why has every man deserted us? Some even ran naked into the night, leaving their garments behind.[49] They had no root. Faithless cowards."

From the edge of the woods, I looked back to watch Joanna join Susanna, Magdalene, and Bathsheba around our once-peaceful campfire. They sat silently with a mixture of grief, anger, and bewilderment on their faces. "Why are we the only ones who did not flee?" Susanna asked. "Are we the only ones with a rooted mustard seed, with good soil?"

I thought about how differently the day had started as I looked cautiously out from behind a rock. The soldiers were gone, so I decided to join the women. They looked at me as if I were a ghost, when I walked up. None of them said a word. I wondered what type of soil I was, where the eleven men had run to, and what we would do now. After a few moments, I walked off to pray alone.

---

[49] Mark 14:50-52

CHAPTER

FIFTEEN

ISOLATION AND FEAR

The next day, the women and I walked into the city. There was no interest in, or time for, breakfast, and we soon fell in with the bustling crowds. Rumors filled the air about what had happened the night before, and about what was to come today. Following the crowds, we soon reached a large courtyard where Jesus stood, bruised and bloodied, next to another man in chains. For Magdalene and Joanna, this sight was as horrific as Herod's bloodshed of the infant boys. I felt ill with knee-buckling fear.

We listened as a man in charge, named Pilate, described the custom of letting one man go free, and that the freed man would be chosen by the people. Pilate was the Roman prefect with the supreme power to judge and execute, and he made it known and very plain that he wanted the people to free Jesus. He asked, "Which one do you want me to release, the innocent teacher, who has done nothing wrong, or Barabbas, the murderous thief?"[50]

Jesus stood next to Barabbas and stared blankly at the crowd, seeming indifferent. I noticed some of the men from our camp, as well as my brother, among the people. Pilate shouted the question again. "Which one will you set free?"

Peter and Thomas and some of the other men stood across the courtyard. None of them spoke up when Pilate asked the question a second time. I later learned that Peter and the others had denied even knowing Jesus when people recognized them. This silent betrayal was the sorrow that had put Jesus on his knees the night before. His distress was in failing us. None of us were good soil when the moment of testing came.

As I stood in silence, I remembered the shouts of joy from the crowds as we entered the city just days before. I felt certain Jesus would be set free, but then I heard someone shout Barabbas's name. I started shouting, "Jesus," in response, and then the four women joined in with the same cry: "Free Jesus."

I could hear Nicodemus in the front row, also yelling, "Free Jesus!" Jesus saw me and the women and Nicodemus, and a look of peace came over his face. I could tell that he felt the presence of his Father, and that perhaps he had not failed us. Suddenly I felt a knife at my throat, and the women and I were dragged from the

---

[50] Matthew 27:17.

screaming crowd by Barabbas's friends. I heard one of the attackers say, "Do not mark her. She will bring a high price." I heard the sounds of fists pounding flesh, and just before I lost consciousness, I realized there was only one small voice shouting Jesus's name. It was Nicodemus.

Susanna was the first to awaken from the beating and found that nothing was broken. It was close to midnight. She looked around for Bathsheba and realized that she had been taken to be sold back into slavery. It was dawn before Joanna, Magdalene, and I were able to move. We noticed doors opening and people walking toward the mountains nearby. Joanna said that she felt ill, and I'm sure the other's shared my thoughts. Where were the men? What happened?

As we walked through the streets in shock, I asked every passer-by if Jesus had been set free. Finally, a young girl replied, "It was Barabbas." I asked her to tell me what she meant, and she responded, "Pilate tried to free the innocent man, yet the crowd demanded his death. Then Pilate flicked water at the Pharisees in the front row and declared that he was innocent of Jesus's blood and that it was their responsibility! My mother took me away, so I do not know what happened next."[51]

I drifted into troubled thought. "Where were the eleven? What has happened? Why did the people not demand that Jesus be spared? Even Nicodemus had cheered for Jesus. Could the other men really still be in hiding?"

What Peter had said yesterday about being poor soil kept

---

[51] Matthew 27:24.

coming back to me. Did Jesus know that this would happen? I vividly saw myself and the others in the parable. I was indeed rocky soil, hearing the word without root and, as predicted, when trouble came, I ran quickly and fell away.

I was getting angry, not only with myself, but with the other men as well. They were also rocky soil, receiving and believing Jesus's teachings with joy, but falling away in the time of testing—literally running away when the soldiers showed up.[52] They fell away before Pilate as well; in fact, most of them denied even knowing Jesus. Rocky soil was the description that fit all of us—each one—and we had been with Jesus for three years! He gave us three years of his life, and now he was giving it all.

Then it hit me: the women were good soil—they did not lack. They had not run; they did not hide. They went to the courtyard, and now they were here. Nicodemus was good soil too. How was this possible? Did I have thorns and weeds flourishing around my rocky soil as well?

---

[52] Luke 8:13.

SIXTEEN

FIRST BREATH

By the time we reached the hilltop, Jesus had been on the cross for some time already. When Joanna broke through the mob, Jesus recognized her and a peaceful look came over him. Magdalene and Susanna soon joined her, and the three women knelt at the foot of the crucifixion cross. I was terrified at the sight of the nails driven through Jesus's hands and feet and saw only the crowd's sanguine eyes as I looked around. None of the eleven were here! How could this be? I gained some courage when I saw Joanna, Magdalene, and Susanna.[53] Susanna's eyes met mine,

---

[53] Mark 15:41.

and I recalled washing her feet. This gave me the strength to join them at the foot of the cross Jesus was nailed to.

I was in shock, and I vowed never to forget or forgive my brothers for this, their third act of betrayal. Then I thought I heard Jesus say, "Father, forgive them, for they do not know what they are doing."[54] I looked up and noticed two others being crucified—how had I not seen them until now? I heard the one nearest Jesus ask to be remembered by him. Jesus said, "Truly I tell you, today you will be with me in paradise."[55]

Then I heard Joanna whisper, "The first will be last, and the last will be first." I thought I understood. This criminal was the last to believe Jesus, and he would be the first to be in the kingdom of God with him. I would ask Joanna later if that was right.

We all looked up at our teacher and heard his calming voice saying, "I am ascending to my Father and your Father, to my God and your God.[56] You are the children of the living God; you do not lack. You have come through the narrow door, through the eye of the needle. Rejoice, for you are good soil." His lips did not move, but the words penetrated our hearts and minds.

"You are my brothers and sisters and mothers, whom I love, and in whom I am well pleased." The sound was Jesus's voice, but it came from within us. With a loud cry, he breathed his last, and I heard a soldier declare, "Surely this man was the Son of God!"

---

[54] Luke 23:34.

[55] Luke 23:43.

[56] John 20:17.

CHAPTER

SEVENTEEN

FOLLOW ME

W e stayed at the crucifixion ground long after Jesus's body was removed and the cross was taken away. There was much grief—paralyzing grief—among us, and we had only each other for support. I thought, *But support to do what? What now?* We just wanted to stay where we sat, at the spot where he was unjustly killed. We couldn't bring ourselves to leave the last place we would ever see Jesus alive or hear his words.

As the sun cracked over the hilltop the next morning, I said, "Follow me." After a brief walk, Magdalene, Susanna, Joanna, and I found ourselves sitting outside of the tomb. Salome, another former slave of Susanna, had also heard me at the cross and followed us.[57] The women were grateful for my having led them to the tomb for final prayers. We sat for hours, grieving the loss of the one who had truly loved us. And we all felt physically ill at the other men's lack of faith. "Where are the men?" Joanna asked. "Why are they not even here at Jesus tomb? They are such cowards."

I replied, "Rocky soil with weeds that choke."

I could not remember my last meal or my last drink—or the last time I had slept—yet I felt fully alive. Jesus's words pierced my heart, and finally, I could see and hear. "Your treasure is where your heart is," Jesus had taught us. I realized that Jesus *was* the treasure, and knowing his belief in me, I would not lack. A feeling of abundance and joy swept over me, and I knew what I had to do.

Three days passed, and I said to the women, "Follow me." The five of us walked toward the sea, and as we did, I spoke about many of Jesus's lessons, even some we had forgotten long ago. It seemed that I did not need Thomas's parchments. The women looked at each other in wonder, and Susanna said with a smile, "We feel the presence of Jesus when you talk and when we simply walk with you."

We traveled for most of the day and then came to a house with an old woman sitting out front. I went in without knocking and the women followed.

---

[57] Mark 15:39.

CHAPTER

EIGHTEEN

COME TOGETHER

We went inside to find most of the men seated around a table that filled the small room. Peter said, "Andrew, praise God that you are here and have found us." I looked at my brother, knowing Peter hoped that I had forgotten the last time we were together, sharing Jesus's Parable of Rocky Soil and Good Soil.

Peter said, "Thomas is in charge of keeping the doors locked. We were all afraid of the Jewish leaders.[58] There is a price on our heads, and we don't want to die."

---

[58] John 20:19.

The others began throwing questions at us, and there was much confusion. Joanna spoke of the arrest, the courtyard, and the cross, and then of the tomb and the pain. "Hold your tongue, woman!" Thomas cried. "You do not understand what dangers we faced, even coming to this house to meet. We do not need to hear from you."

I silenced him, saying, "Joanna, Magdalene, Susanna, and Salome will speak as they will, for they did not flee into the night at the first sign of trouble, as you did. You will listen." They looked at each other in amazement. "What has happened to Andrew?" Peter whispered. "He speaks with authority!" It surprised me as well. I had been transformed into good soil, into the butterfly. Fear of humanity and the desires of this world no longer held the women or me captive.

The men listened as Joanna looked each one in the eye and said, "You are to carry Jesus's parables and deeds to all who will listen. Pray that they have ears to hear and eyes to see."

After Joanna had finished speaking, I asked everyone to gather around and stand with me, holding hands and saying, "You are all children of the living God. Bow your heads and let us pray together." The house cried out loudly as we had been taught by Jesus, saying with one voice, "Our Father, hallowed be your name, your kingdom come, your will be done, on earth as it is in heaven. Give us today our daily bread. And forgive us our debts, as we also have forgiven our debtors. And lead us not into temptation but deliver us from our evil desires.[59] May we say and live this prayer daily in memory of you."

I looked to heaven and then to the others, saying, "We are no more of this world than Jesus.[60] None of you lack, unless you deny yourself. You have all come through the narrow door, through the eye of the needle, and you are good soil. Do not conform to any of the patterns of this world. You are my brothers and sisters and mothers, whom our Father loves, and in whom he is well pleased. Jesus was sent, and now he sends us." Everyone looked at me in amazement, except Joanna, who seemed filled with warmth and safety.

I said, "We will meet here in a week and go forth to proclaim the good news."

"But, Teacher," Peter said.

I sharply silenced my older brother, telling him, "None are to be called *teacher*, for you have one teacher, and he is with us and gives us the words and power. You are in him, and you are all brothers, our Father's children."[61]

---

[59] Matthew 6:9.
[60] John 17:16.
[61] Matthew 23:8.

CHAPTER

NINETEEN

THE ELEVENTH

A week later, we gathered at the house in late evening. All but Judas were there. No one had seen or heard from him since Jesus's crucifixion.

The women and I planned to leave the next morning to share the good news where fertile soil could be found. We hoped to travel to all cities and villages outside of Jerusalem. I commanded everyone else to go into the city. "Go after dark, and go through the eye of the needle to strengthen yourself in memory and power. When you are crossing through the narrow door, stop and commit to Jesus. When you are hungry, remember that your food is to do the will of our Father who sent Jesus, and when you are weary, believe in

Jesus's ways, taking his yoke upon yourself and leaning on him. Then you will find rest for your souls."[62]

After that, I prayed, "Father, help us rely upon you as our teacher did. In times of trouble, when we don't know what to say, help us trust that it will be you speaking, your Spirit.[63] Help us find peace when we are arrested and brought to trial and not to worry about what we are to say. Test our faith in your time and as you will in order to help us mature and not lack, as we know it will be you and not us speaking.[64] Let your light shine through us and before others and help us continue to till and weed our soil, as your will desires. Let others see your deeds through us and glorify you, Father."[65]

"The kingdom of God is within you.[66] Now, go with peace!" I told them.

As I was turning to leave, Thomas said, "Judas has not returned, and we need to add to our group. There are twelve tribes to be accounted for in heaven."

The women and I spent the night at the house before setting out early the next morning. When I opened the door, I saw a young man standing by the side of the road. He had piercing blue eyes that made the rags he wore and the smell of swine that surrounded him nearly unnoticeable. I approached him and said, "Go into that

---

[62] Mathew 11:29.
[63] Matthew 10:20.
[64] Mark 13:11.
[65] Mathew 5:16.
[66] Luke 17:21.

house and relay your poem to those inside." He did, and we listened from outside.

"My name is Matthias," the young man said. "A man just came up to me outside of your house and told me to come inside and relay my poem to those who can hear. I do not understand how he knew of my poem, as it came in a dream that woke me only a few minutes ago! How is this possible? Do you know who that man is? Was he a prophet?"

Thomas said, "Recite your poem," and so Matthias began.

> In the early dew, I seek your face,
> The face I looked for while others were in a dream.
> I sought you with eyes open and closed, but you could not
> be found.
> I longed for your touch in the day, in the sky, and by the sea;
> I felt you, your presence, but could not hold on.
> As I lay gazing at the starry canvas, simply enjoying the view,
> There you were with a thousand eyes.
> Whom I sought had been found;
> There was no need to touch or see, as we ineffably were.
> We were one; you gave me what was asked.
> Overwhelmed and connected to all—past, present, and future.
> How did I get here? And then you were gone.
> Tears of joy sprang forth for the presence of you,
> Tears of sadness for the separation;
> I no longer cry out for this union; you are here.
> I am in you, as your will desires, if I but surrender.

Young Matthias begged, "Please, what does the dream mean? Who was that stranger, and why am I here?"

Peter said, "Tell us the name of your poem."

"Journey," Mathias replied.

No one noticed that the women and I were standing outside. I whispered, "We have been on this journey with Jesus for the past three years."

I stepped inside and told Matthias of Jesus's prayer to our God— and now his God, "I pray that all of them may be one, Father, just as you are in me and I am in you, may they also be in us."[67] The men were all astounded that Matthias's poem ended with *I am in you*.

Peter shouted, "Do you see? The words *I am in you* is the transformation that we must make. We only need to accept the love that God has offered. In exchange, we give up the things of this world."

Matthias was confused and frightened, which he would be for some time. But Jesus's prayer was fulfilled with Matthias, and he joined the ten of us and went to the eye of the needle after dark to bring Jesus's message to Jerusalem.

---

[67] John 17:20–21.

CHAPTER

TWENTY

SAUL EMERGES AS PAUL

S ometimes when the women asked me a question, I would say, "The answer is in the wind." I would smile, remembering Jesus telling Nicodemus, "The wind blows wherever it pleases. You hear its sound, but you cannot tell where it comes from or where it is going and so it is with those reborn of the Spirit."[68]

The women and I walked where the wind blew, and we ended up on the road to Ephesus. This was one of the most treacherous roads in the region for us to travel. Much blood had been spilled along this walk as the Jewish ruling council offered Roman soldiers

---

[68] John 3.

bounty on Jesus's followers; the most ruthless was rumored to be a Roman soldier named Saul.

Suddenly, the women froze. Just ahead, a family was being beheaded. The sight and sounds of it were unimaginable and would haunt me for the rest of my life. As we walked closer, the women looked to me for guidance. I kept walking toward the slaughter but motioned for them not to follow.

The soldier looked at us curiously, "More sheep and more coin for my pocket," he said, laughing.

I walked to within a foot of his drawn blade and asked, "What is your name?"

"I am Saul, and your heads will soon add to my purse."

"You are orphaned," I told the soldier. "Our teacher is a man from Nazareth, accredited by God to do miracles, wonders, and signs, which God will do and say to you this hour through him, as you now know![69] It is written, our God, and now your God, declared, 'I will raise up a prophet from among the people, and I will put my words in his mouth, and he will tell them everything I command.' Our teacher is now with you, and you are in him."[70]

The grin slipped from Saul's face, and he suddenly looked helpless. Although blood still dripped from his blade, he was unable to move.

Susanna stepped forward and placed her hands over Saul's face. "When you open your eyes, you will be transformed, and you will know our Father's love, will, and purpose for your life. You will no

---

[69] Acts 2:22.

[70] Deuteronomy 18:15–18.

longer be Saul, and you will no longer conform to the patterns of this world. You are a new creation and shall be called Paul. When you open your eyes, you will be able to test and approve of our Father's will for your life. Our Father is God Almighty!"[71]

Paul's eyes remained closed as we walked, and Susanna guided his steps. That night, we stayed in an open shelter just outside of Ephesus. Around nightfall, Paul opened his eyes for the first time and then slept the sleep of the dead without a word.

---

[71] Romans 12:2.

CHAPTER

TWENTY-ONE

EPHESUS

T he dew was heavy the next morning, but the sun would make quick work of it. The women had gone to the town baker shortly before daylight, and the scent of fresh bread was in the air. Paul came to me and asked, "What happened to me yesterday?" The women giggled when I turned away without answering. I walked off to pray by myself and to find a house worthy of our peace.

Joanna asked Susanna to help Salome bring the parchments and papyrus they had copied and stored in water vases. Paul looked troubled, and the women knew why.

Susanna read the Parable of the Lost Son out loud and shared how the father had looked upon his two boys, the obedient and the lost, with equanimity. She ended by saying, "It is written in the law that your God and Father wants your heart to discover the teachings of Jesus and to know that God blots out all of your past transgressions, for his own sake, and remembers your sins no more.[72] In time, you will learn to see yourself as our Father sees you."

I said, "Follow me."

After a short walk from last night's shelter, we were welcomed into a one-room house. We stayed there for several months, and Paul grew into his role as a teacher of God's Word. The crowds of people wanting to hear the good news grew larger each day. They waited every night outside of the house for Paul's familiar words, "Greetings to God's people in Ephesus, by the will of God, grace and peace to you from God our Father and my brothers and sisters. May you be blessed with and may you receive every blessing." He then told them of his experience on the road just outside of town, adding," Let those with ears to hear, hear, and those with eyes to see, see." Susanna would then hand Paul a parchment to read, and Paul colored the parables with his own flare. Saul had been the scribe and orator for the queen, and his delivery inspired and sometimes confused people, just as Jesus's had.

One day, an hour before the usual time, people started to gather to be close to the front and to hear Paul spread Jesus's words. I said, "Follow me," and everyone gathered their things. There was some confusion, but we recalled walking from town to village with Jesus,

---

[72] Isaiah 43:25.

hearing the familiar words, "Go without purse, bag or sandals, and you will lack nothing!"

Salome and Magdalene said they were going to stay in Ephesus and continue reading from the parchments. The first permanent nightly gatherings were established in Ephesus. The rest of our group walked down the road toward Philippi.

TWENTY-TWO

TIMOTHY

As we approached the outskirts of town, Paul stopped. He saw the town drunk sleeping in the gutter, using a wine bottle for a pillow. The gutter drained the waste from the village. Susanna intuitively felt directed to a parchment, which she handed to Paul. She put her hands on the poor man's face as Paul read the words. "Who has woe? Who has sorrow? Who has strife? Who has complaints? Who has needless bruises? Who has bloodshot eyes? Who has a bottle for a pillow? Those who linger over wine, who go to sample bowls of mixed wine. Do not gaze at wine when it is red, when it sparkles in the cup, when it goes down smoothly. In the end it bites like a snake and poisons like a viper. Your eyes will see strange sights, and your mind will imagine confusing things."

The drunkard stirred slightly, and Paul continued to read. "You will be like one sleeping on the high seas, lying on top of the rigging. 'They hit me,' you will say, 'but I'm not hurt! They beat me, but I don't feel it! When will I wake up so I can find another drink?'"[73]

Memories of my dad's drinking came back to me. When my mother would fuss at him, the reply was always, "Good day or bad day, rain or shine, there is always time for wine."

Paul shouted, "Father, lift our brother's desire for drink and pleasure, where it is never found. Farmer, cast out the weeds growing in our brother." He then looked at the man, the glaze in his eyes had cleared, and asked his name. "Timothy," he replied. Paul stood and said, "Follow me."

We spent the night in the barn of a man named Philemon, who, by chance, had been a close childhood friend of our new companion, Timothy. Paul read Jesus's parable of the lost and obedient son. Timothy and Philemon listened intently since they had taken very different paths in life. Each saw himself and the other in the parable, and they were changed forever. Timothy and Philemon told their friends to meet at the barn at sunset to hear the travelers talk about God. The appointed hour came, and Paul opened the barn door, welcoming everyone with the familiar words, "Greetings to God's holy people of Philippi, by the will of God, grace and peace be in you from our Father, God, and my

---

[73] Proverbs 23:19.

brothers and sisters. May you be blessed to hear teachings of our teacher and receive the spirit."[74] Paul asked those who traveled near Ephesus to send greetings to Salome and Magdalene, and he always closed the gathering with, "Let those with ears to hear, hear and those with eyes to see, see!"

Susanna seemed to intuitively know the right teaching to hand Paul each evening, and soon the Philippians were spreading the news to one another. The barn was more crowded than ever imagined possible. Philemon asked to read the parchment that evening, and Paul and Timothy smiled with encouragement.

Somewhere along the way, Susanna had fallen in love with Paul—something only Paul knew. She dared not share her secret with the other women. She feared their reaction to what had happened. Her heart wanted what it wanted, and she wondered if a mustard seed or a weed was growing inside.

The next evening, though a storm was brewing and there was lightning was in the distance, the townspeople started to show up at the barn. I told the group to follow me, and we prepared to walk to the next town. I told Timothy and Philemon to stay at the barn and do the regular evening readings. Timothy and Philemon decided to read the Parable of the Lost and Obedient Son on the eve of each full moon and to continue the work of God in Philippi. We left a copy of each parchment with them, and this was the beginning of another permanent gathering site. Timothy would write to Paul with any questions or difficulties.

---

[74] Philippians 1.

CHAPTER

TWENTY-THREE

MORE ROCKY SOIL

J ust before we left for Ephesus, Paul asked me if we might have a private word. There was pain in his voice, and it crackled as he shared his secret with me in a low whisper. "I know that Jesus's word is spirit and truth. I must be unspiritual. I do not understand what I do. For what I want to do I do not do, but what I hate to do, I do. I have the desire to do what is good, but I cannot carry it out. I do not do the good I want to do, but the evil I do not want to do. This I keep on doing! Although I want to do good, evil desire is right there with me![75] How can this be, Andrew?" he asked.

---

[75] Romans 7:15–22.

"I am a prisoner of my own desire. My desire is for Susanna, and it overwhelms me nightly."

I loved Paul and told him, "It takes time to turn a good intention into a transformed way of living." I turned to leave so Paul could consider my words when Joanna appeared with two parchments.

"Paul, let me tell you the meaning of the Parable of Lack," she said. She sat with Paul and spoke of the eleven men crouching down to walk through the eye of the needle doorway at the Jerusalem wall. She explained that the men had clearly seen themselves in Jesus's parable when the guard shouted, "Leave all weapons outside, if you wish to enter. They finally realized that the weapons they carried to protect them actually put them in a prison."

Joanna continued, "They received this meaning very quickly and knew that seeking worldly pleasures would put them in prison too. The men finally saw that to enter the kingdom of God, they must give up everything to go through the narrow door, and that willingness to do so was what they lacked. They wore some pleasures and protections like a comfortable, old garment—when they held onto those, they discovered that they remained in lack.

"At that time, the Parable of the Farmer had not deeply rooted in my heart, and so it is with you now. I have brought a copy of the parable so that you might read to yourself after we have left. The Parable of the Farmer is meant to remind us to keep our ears open and our eyes clear. The soil lacks because it contains evil desires and things of this world, and the soil is everyone. The rocky soil, or soil with thorns, needs constant and continuous tending by the farmer. With man, this is impossible. Paul, you are the soil. With the farmer, all things are possible."

Joanna saw no clarity in Paul's eyes, so she continued. "The thorns, weeds, and rocks are the patterns and desires of this world, valued in the eyes of man and growing everywhere, yet detestable in the sight of the farmer, who is your heavenly Father! To enter the kingdom, your cost is all the weeds, thorns, and rocks—especially those desires that you covet the most! You must ask that your desire for the pleasure you covet to be removed by the farmer. You must be willing to have the weeds thrown into the fire, along with the secret pleasures that choke you."

Joanna remembered what Magdalene had said: "A weed is any desire of man—anything that prevents you from seeing clearly. You will not lack when you truly know yourself. When Saul is dead, Paul will fly in freedom, as it is with the caterpillar and the butterfly. Only then will you realize the assurance of being a beloved son of your Father. If you do not know yourself and who you are, you will continue to dwell in poverty and corruption—for it will be you who are that poverty, that rocky soil!"[76]

Joanna asked Paul, "What would change if you viewed service to God as the only goal the rest of your life?" Joanna turned to me and took my hand, and we walked away to find Susanna and the others, leaving Paul to his thoughts. He would have to make a decision.

---

[76] Thomas 3.

TWENTY-FOUR

THE GOOD SOIL

After we left, Paul sat alone in the rain with his thoughts. Joanna's words stayed with him, and he knew his purpose was to live only to share the words of Jesus with anyone who would listen—no matter the peril. Paul spent the night in solitude and silence in the open field and left the next morning for the nearby town of Corinth. Paul took only a copy of the parchments for his journey.

Months passed, and Paul unceasingly vowed to stay in the will of God and be the good soil. He was tired of merely trying to be a good man and decided he truly wanted to be one. He kept reminding himself that with the aid of his Father, all things were possible. Paul did as I had taught him: he found a worthy house and put Jesus's peace upon its dwellers. As Paul asked for God's strength, he no longer did what he did not want to do; instead, he did only what he wanted to do. His desires for God overtook his desires of the flesh.

In Corinth, Paul went to the house of Crispus, the loud and rather-round leader of the local synagogue. Paul did not yet feel comfortable entering a synagogue, and so he continued to speak every night from outside of Crispus's home. Many of the Corinthians who heard Paul believed, and after a time, he left a copy of his scrolls behind and moved on to the next town.

He walked from town to village to farmhouse, sharing the good news; and each time he decided it was time to move on, he remembered to leave everything behind—his purse, extra food, and clothing. The only thing he kept were copies of the parchments—the mustard seeds, as everyone seemed to be calling them now. Walking alone on the road, Paul had never felt so abundant and connected. He had, without knowing how or when, begun to store up his treasure in heaven, even while still on the earth.

Paul stayed with Aquila in Antioch for a while and continud reading the parchments nightly and sharing the story of a man named Saul who was reborn as Paul. Paul's next stop was Cilicia, located on the northern border of Rome, for a few weeks. He stayed in the house of a woman named Priscilla. Soon, Pricilla was leading the evening gatherings and reading the mustard seeds.

Everywhere Paul went, meetings were held in people's houses until they overflowed, and Paul began to see his life's purpose clearly. He was gladly drinking from the cup his Father had handed him. He knew he would head for Rome next.

CHAPTER

TWENTY-FIVE

LOVE FOUND AND LOST

When we left Paul that day, sitting in the rain, Susanna was heartbroken. She wept at leaving him behind. Had she known that it would be the last time we would see Paul alive, she might not have followed us. Her love for Paul was deep and wide, and she was now carrying his child.

As we traveled, news of Paul's work and the successful establishment of so many nightly gatherings reached us. Susanna's hopes of being in the same town as Paul were her constant companion.

Our travels took us to the outskirts of Rome, but I surprised Joanna and Susanna by saying, "Follow me." They looked at each other curiously. We had just arrived at the gates of Rome, and for weeks, I had done nothing but speak of the work that must be done there. They assumed we would be in Rome through the harvest season.

I told them we were heading back to Jerusalem to see how the eleven were faring. I had heard no news from them in months and feared they had become soil filled with rocks and weeds. After saying "Follow me," I never explained my reasoning behind the decision, just as Jesus had done. The women found my words unsettling, but I knew the more urgent reason to leave Rome. Paul was imprisoned there.

As we were leaving the city, a troubled messenger found us and relayed the news that I had feared we would hear. He said, "Paul has been in prison for months. The Pharisee that hired Saul and paid him to kill Jesus's followers discovered that Paul and Saul were the same man. The Pharisee learned of Paul's scheduled release today, and he paid to have another prisoner stab Paul to try to finally put an end to Jesus. His cell is to be emptied later today." Before the messenger could express his sadness, a loud wail pierced our ears.

"I must see his body!" Susanna cried.

There was no stopping her, and I prayed silently, "Father, news of Paul appears to be very bad. But we know that you love us, and this is in our best interest and yours. I ask, and only if it is your will, that you please someday reveal to us why Paul was killed."

The women went to the prison to claim Paul's body and to give him a proper burial, but his body was gone when they arrived. Susanna insisted on seeing the cell, and the guard took pity on the pregnant woman. Joanna accompanied her. It was damp, and the smell of blood filled the air. Joanna noticed a large pile of papyrus—letters in Paul's hand. They were Paul's answers to the people who had written him about their troubles with brothers and sisters and also his interpretations of the mustard seeds and parables.

The replies began with the same words that Paul used in his nightly messages to the crowds, and Joanna smiled as she glanced through them. She realized Paul's flare, which took the Parable of Lack and the Parable of the Sower to new depths. She read,

> Therefore, brothers and sisters, we have an obligation to live according to the teaching. See yourself in the parable, for if you live according to your desires, thorns and rocks will lead to death. If you live by the Spirit, you put to death your desires and misdeeds. When you know yourself, you will become known, and you will realize that you are the children of the living God. For those who are led by the Spirit of God are the children of God. The Spirit you receive brings about your adoption by our Father, and Jesus's word testifies that we are God's children and coheirs with Jesus in the kingdom of God.[77]

Joanna knew that the letters she held were most precious and gathered them all together. Susanna, still weeping by the bed, was overwhelmed and paid no attention, never seeing what Joanna

---

[77] Romans 8:12–17.

held. We met later that evening, and Joanna shared Paul's writings with us all. I studied them by the fire. At daybreak I arose and said, "Follow me." I left for Jerusalem with everyone except the three women who had accompanied me.

Susanna and Joanna stayed in Rome for a time to continue sharing what they had been given. I knew that this was now their life's desire and purpose—their cup. They made many copies of the parchments Joanna had saved, and soon Paul's new writings were dispersed throughout the land.

Eventually, Joanna asked the women to follow her, and they set off for Ephesus, seeking Magdalene and Salome, with copies of three responses from Paul. Along the way, Susanna read the letters aloud to her unborn child, Paul's child. I joined them on the third day of the journey, and we built a fire near the old olive tree and stream where we had spent so many nights with Jesus. There were still signs of the old camp where we had stayed earlier in the year, though it seemed a lifetime ago. With trembling hands, Joanna handed a partial, torn scroll to Susanna. This one had not been copied, and only the top half was found. Tears formed in her eyes as Susanna recognized Paul's hand.

My prison release comes tomorrow, unexpectedly. It has given me grave concern, so I write the unspoken words that I pray find you well and fall on your heart. Should my time arrive before our eyes again meet, know that my last breath whispers Susanna. Rejoice for me, for I await my time to emerge from this earthly body, as I would await our child from your womb, had we been so blessed. Our one night of feasting has left me with no regrets of this life. Each night I remember how beautiful you are! Your eyes, your hair, your smell, your lips, your mouth - all are lovely. There is no flaw. You stole my heart.

Susanna placed the scroll upon her breast. I could nearly hear her heart beating across the fire. She blushed, remembering the moment when Paul and she walked away from camp in silence. She smiled at Joanna, then drifted into sleep.

I decided to slip away from camp to pray in solitude as my teacher had done. As I prayed, I reflected on all of the teachings and experiences of the past three and a half years. I was at peace and had assurance that God loved me. My purpose, my cup, was to lead the twelve to a total dependency on our Father. I could think of no better will for my life.

The next morning, we started the day as we had for the past three years, by saying the prayer Jesus taught us. Susanna added a request for God to help deliver Paul's replies to the many towns he had written to while in prison, the first one being Ephesus. As we walked along the dusty road, we each felt complete and mature. We lacked nothing. There was only one thing left to do: choose a fitting name for Paul's son, who was also the great-great-grandson of Solomon from the line of David.

EPILOGUE

I secretly visited with Paul in the Roman prison the day before his death. Initially it was a joyous meeting, and he told of the many towns he had stayed in and how he moved on to the next town once the nightly gatherings were established. It was clear that Paul had succeeded more than any of the twelve in sharing the teachings of Jesus and producing good soil, and I asked him why he thought this was so. He replied; "Do you remember Joanna's parting question to me the night before you left Ephesus? 'What would change if I view service to God as the goal in all my decisions and actions?' That question helped me answer my life's purpose." Paul asked, "Do you recall our last conversation?"

"Yes, I do," I said. "Have you found peace to your questions?"

Paul replied, "Yes. I was convinced that I must be unspiritual. For what I wanted to do I did not do. What I hated to do, I did. I had the knowledge of what was right and the desire to do what was good, but I failed at carrying it out. I asked myself how I could have all this knowledge and preach God's Word with such conviction, but yet have my desires overwhelm me when I least expect it?"

Paul continued, "The night you left, I was on my knees, pounding the wet earth and begging God to help me see and hear the answer. I wept as the rain continued, and when I felt hopeless and without options, God spoke. 'You do not ask me for the power to do what is good and for the power not to do what isn't. Knowledge is necessary, yet insufficient.' I found that I could carry out good practices for a period, and then I would fail. I also found that, for a period, I would stop doing what I know is evil, and then I would fail. Our Father's answer was so simple and rang so true. What do you think?"

I reflected on this for a moment before answering. "At each critical moment, all of the men in our group failed Jesus. Even now, they are not doing the work in Jerusalem that you have been doing in all the other towns. We failed when we went out to put our peace upon others' homes, and Jesus declared that we lacked faith. "You only need the mustard seed," he would proclaim. Jesus must have been saying that we only needed a small amount of God's power and we would succeed. Clearly, we did not ask for the power from our Father to do what Jesus sent us out to do. My eyes have been opened, and now I can see. I will tell Joanna and Susanna about viewing service to God as the goal and asking for His power, although they seem to have been doing just that. We are camped just outside of town."

Paul was alarmed and matter-of-factly stated, "You must take the women from Rome immediately, as I may not see another sunrise." Before I could protest, he said, "The time of my departure has come. I have fought the good fight, I have finished the race and I have kept the faith. This is the cup our Father handed me, and I gladly drink from it. I am not of this world, and neither are you."

---

2 Timothy 4:7

A SPECIAL NOTE ABOUT SCRIPTURAL REFERENCES:

Unless otherwise mentioned, the quoted or paraphrased wording throughout the book uses the NIV translation. Other scriptural references can be found on the web and some are provided below for easy reference.

Second Logion: "Jesus said, Except you fast to the world, you shall in no way find the kingdom of God.'"

Gospel of Thomas

3. Jesus said, "If your leaders say to you, 'Look, the (Father's) kingdom is in the sky,' then the birds of the sky will precede you. If they say to you, 'It is in the sea,' then the fish will precede you. Rather, the (Father's) kingdom is within you, and it is outside you.

When you know yourselves, then you will be known, and you will understand that you are children of the living Father. But if you do not know yourselves, then you live in poverty, and you are the poverty.

9. Jesus said, "Look, the sower went out, took a handful (of seeds), and scattered (them). Some fell on the road, and the birds came and gathered them. Others fell on rock, and they didn't take root in the soil and didn't produce heads of grain. Others fell on

thorns, and they choked the seeds and worms ate them. And others fell on good soil, and it produced a good crop: it yielded sixty per measure and one hundred twenty per measure."

46. Jesus said, "From Adam to John the Baptist, among those born of women, no one is so much greater than John the Baptist that his eyes should not be averted. But I have said that whoever among you becomes a child will recognize the (Father's) kingdom and will become greater than John."

67. Jesus said, "Those who know all, but are lacking in themselves, are utterly lacking."

90. Jesus said, "Come to me, for my yoke is comfortable and my lordship is gentle, and you will find rest for yourselves."

99. The disciples said to him, "Your brothers and your mother are standing outside."

He said to them, "Those here who do what my Father wants are my brothers and my mother. They are the ones who will enter my Father's kingdom."

ABOUT THE AUTHOR

David Schofield is a retired actuary and business broker. He is the father of two wonderful children. His passion is to bring others into a relationship and dependency on God. David resides in Centerdale, Rhode Island. This is his first book.